Survival
Prepping

T0064848

Survival
Prepping

A Guide to Hunkering Down, Bugging Out, and Getting Out of Dodge

Jason Ryder Adams

Skyhorse Publishing

Skyhorse Publishing books may be purchased in bulk at special discounts for sales promotion, corporate gifts, fund-raising, or educational purposes. Special editions can also be created to specifications. For details, contact the Special Sales Department, Skyhorse Publishing, 307 West 36th Street, 11th Floor, New York, NY 10018 or info@skyhorsepublishing.com.

Skyhorse® and Skyhorse Publishing® are registered trademarks of Skyhorse Publishing, Inc.®, a Delaware corporation.

Visit our website at www.skyhorsepublishing.com.

10 9 8 7 6 5 4 3 2 1

Library of Congress Cataloging-in-Publication Data is available on file.

Cover design by Tom Lau
Cover photo credit: iStockphoto.com

Print ISBN: 978-1-5107-3611-5
Ebook ISBN: 978-1-5107-3612-2

Printed in the United States of America

Contents

Why Survival Prepping?

NO ONE KNOWS WHAT IT WILL BE.

It could be a natural disaster or a medical pandemic. Financial system collapse or bioterrorism. Governmental shutdown or societal breakdown. The media are full of possible threats, and they seem to be coming at us from all sides these days.

No one knows WHEN it will be.

It might be today or tomorrow. Next week or next month. Next year . . . or maybe never.

But do you want to take a chance on "maybe never"?

It pays to be prepared. "Prepare for the worst, pray for the best," as the saying goes. And if there ever was a time to prepare for the worst, NOW is that time.

"Survival prepping" is about preparing for the worst. It's about making sure you and your family are safe, no matter what the world throws at you.

It used to be that "preppers" were looked at as paranoid by those who were being polite, or as whackos or nut cases by those who weren't.

But look at the events of recent years: Natural disasters such as Hurricanes Katrina, Sandy, Harvey, Florence, and Michael. Man-made disasters such as Japan's nuclear meltdown. Economic crises like those in Europe. Unemployment, work shortages, and financial crises in the United States all within the last 15 years.

Even rioting in the US has become a regular occurrence. We've had multiple incidents of riots and civil unrest over the last few years—in Brooklyn, NY; Baltimore, MD; Los Angeles, CA; Charlotte, NC; Charlottesville, VA; Oakland, CA; and close to home for me, Portland, OR. That's to name but a few.

And it's not just in big cities. Even America's heartland has seen riots, such as those in Michigan (2012), Missouri (2014), and Wisconsin (twice, in 2011 and 2016). Thanks to social media, we must now be prepared for coordinated protests and unrest, such as the antigovernment protests of 2016 that occurred simultaneously in twenty-five cities.

All of these events have helped bring survival prepping out of the fringe and into the mainstream. After all, if you care about your family, you want to make sure they are safe, secure, and thoroughly taken care of, no matter what situation comes your way.

Missing Teeth and Questionable Hygiene

When most people picture a "survivalist," they think of a big, hairy man living alone in a cabin in the woods, wearing camouflage. With missing teeth and questionable hygiene, our stereotypical survivalist clutches his rifle, ready to shoot any "revenooers" and government agents who head his way, all while muttering under his breath that the sooner civilization collapses, the better.

Let me assure you, the stereotype couldn't be further from the truth.

Most of us "survivalist preppers" are ordinary people. We're your neighbors, your coworkers, and your friends. You see us at our kids' soccer games, the neighborhood movie theater, or your local restaurant. You see us at work and church. You see us walking in the neighborhood or exercising at the gym.

We are regular folks living regular lives. I live in a regular house, not a cabin in the woods. I don't hunt and forage all day. Instead, I have a white-collar job in an office, and I shop at the local grocery store. I don't own a single piece of camouflage clothing. And I have all my teeth.

Prepping today isn't for weird nutcases. It's for everyone.

Because the bottom line is, neither you nor I knows what will happen. It might be a natural disaster. It just might be a terrorist act. It might be martial law and civil unrest. Whatever happens, as preppers, we want to be sure that our family is safe and secure.

Survival Insurance

The sane way to look at prepping is to think of it like auto insurance.

You don't buy auto insurance hoping to get into an accident. But the coverage is there because, well, accidents happen, don't they? And you want to be protected in case an accident does occur.

It's the same with survival prepping. You don't prep hoping a disaster happens. You prep hoping it doesn't. You prep because you'll sleep better at night, knowing you and your family have that insurance against the unforeseen.

By the way, I know that every once in a while, you'll see a media story that portrays EVERY survivalist as if they were hoping for a disaster to happen, or even working to cause them!

I doubt this has ever been the case, but even if it has, the media are out of step with the times. Prepping is now mainstream.

As for today's preppers, we are merely those who are concerned enough about our families to want to make sure they are safe. And we do something about it.

If you want to be fully prepared for any emergency that might come your way, there are three major plans you'll need in place. You'll need a *Hunkering Down* plan, a *Get Out of Dodge* plan, and a *Sealing In* plan.

Part 1: Hunkering Down

In part one of this book, we'll focus on your *Hunkering Down* plan. This plan is for situations where you would be forced to stay in your home during an emergency.

Now, when something like a natural disaster strikes, the first thought most people have is evacuation. And there is no doubt that "bugging out" may be your safest option when a catastrophe occurs.

But what if you had no warning of the disaster and couldn't bug out? Or what if the disaster destroys all of your possible escape routes? What if you need to stay in your home for a short while before you can safely bug out?

That's where your *Hunkering Down* plan comes in.

To help you develop this plan, we're going to focus on one particular scenario—the natural disaster. During a natural disaster, you might need to survive for a few days or a few weeks in your home before you can leave or before help arrives—if it ever does arrive!

But don't let our focus on "natural disaster" scenarios fool you. You might hunker down for any number of reasons. No matter what happens that requires you to "bug in," your *Hunkering Down* plan will get you through even the toughest situations.

This section contains easy-to-read, direct, to-the-point chapters on the essentials of hunkering down: how to make sure your home is secure, food storage and preparation, water storage and purification, hygiene, first aid, and communications.

Part 2: Get Out of Dodge

Hunkering down or bugging in is all about making sure you have enough supplies and emergency gear if you need to stay in your home during an emergency.

Bugging out is the opposite. It's all about making sure you have enough supplies and emergency gear ready to take with you if you need to evacuate your home.

The second part of this book focuses on your *GOOD ("Get Out Of Dodge")* plan. You'll discover how to prep yourself and your family for evacuation. Having a *GOOD* plan is just as important as having a hunker-down plan.

We'll help you make the right choices for your *GOOD* plan. We'll discuss bug-out supplies, methods, and locations, plus special considerations for bugging out with children and pets.

Part 3: Sealing In

Of all the things we prep for, there's nothing scarier than biological/chemical disasters. Whether it's an act of deliberate bioterrorism, a rampant pandemic, or an accidental biohazard release, we want to be able to survive no matter what happens.

Your third plan, your *Sealing In* plan, is an extension of your hunker-down plan. It specifically focuses on what you'll need to be prepared for biochemical disasters that might happen. We'll discuss the supplies and procedures you'll need to know for these scenarios. But more important, we'll focus on the mind-set you'll need to develop to survive these scary scenarios.

Part 4: Situational Prepping

Besides your prepping plans for hunkering down, bugging out, or sealing in, you also need instructions on how to survive specific situations. So in part four of this book, we'll look at a few specific prepping scenarios that are becoming more prevalent in the modern world. We'll discuss "situational awareness" in general, but we'll also talk about surviving mass shootings, terrorist attacks, riots, and even difficult police encounters. We'll explore prepping for bigger situations such as financial collapse, cyberattacks, and EMP (electromagnetic pulse) strikes. Plus we'll cover some weather survival situations that are becoming more common, such as extreme cold and extreme heat.

Part 5: Home Security and Weapons

In part five, we'll discuss some of the particular challenges preppers face with home security. Of course, there are steps you can take to keep your family and property safe every day, but disasters and times of upheaval require another level of care. By upping your security for these more extreme times, you'll also be making everyday life much safer for you and your family. To help you do that, we'll discuss home security, firearms, and firearm alternatives.

My Challenge to You

The book is written to help you as a new prepper get started. It's for men and women who care about the safety and welfare of their families.

If you are ready to take those first few steps on the prepper path, this book will help you ensure your family survives, and maybe even thrives, should a disaster strike.

Before I close this introduction, I want to speak honestly here.

I know some of you will read this introduction and still be uncertain whether you should buy this book or not.

You might be reluctant to spend the money on this book—even though the return on your investment in this book (that is, keeping your family safe) is ultimately priceless.

From that standpoint, the few bucks for this book really are a small price to pay.

But if you are still uncertain, here's an experiment you can try to see if you need this book.

Later today, or first thing tomorrow, shut off all the utilities in your home. Shut off your water at the mains. Turn off your electricity at the circuit breaker. Turn off your natural gas. Switch off your phones, internet, and cable.

Now, for the next few hours, you and your family are not to leave your home.

You have to stay right where you are.

Have no contact with the outside world.

How well would you cope?

Could you feed your family?

Would you have enough water for them to drink?

How will you handle them going to the bathroom, and washing and bathing?

How would you find out what's going on during the emergency?

What if your spouse or your child becomes injured? What medical problems could you handle?

What tools and emergency items do you already have at hand?

And most important, do you have the information you need to get through this crisis?

I know most of you won't try this experiment. I think you should, though. It will tell you a lot about how prepared you are.

But if you don't try it, at least imagine doing it. Imagine going through all the motions of daily life without access to utilities, computers, or cell phones. How well would you and your family survive in this situation?

If you are confident you'd do well, if you have all the emergency items you need, plus the know-how to use them, then you don't need this book.

But if you are uncertain, or have questions, or if even the thought of doing this experiment scares you, it's OK. This book can help.

Together, we can put you on the right path to removing that fear and uncertainty. In a short time, we can get you and your family ready to hunker down, bug out, or seal in—no matter what disaster or catastrophe happens.

My Hope for You and Your Family

Let me share with you something personal about writing this book. Most authors, when they write a book, hope you'll find ways to use what they've written.

But I might be one of the few authors who hope you NEVER have to use anything I've written here. Yes, I want you to get your supplies and have your plans together. But I sincerely hope you never actually have to USE them.

I want you to have all this, so that like me, you'll sleep better at night, knowing your family is ready for whatever comes your way.

I sincerely hope you and your family are always safe and have long, healthy, disaster-free lives.

Thank you for your support.

—Jason Ryder Adams
Forest Grove, Oregon

As preppers, we want to be sure that our families are safe and secure, no matter what happens.

PART 1

Hunkering Down: Prepping to Survive in Your Home during a Natural Disaster

What to Expect from a Natural Disaster

THE CORNERSTONE OF YOUR SURVIVAL PREPAREDNESS IS YOUR *Hunker Down* plan.

You can hunker down for any number of reasons, and everything in the first part of this book will help you "bug in" no matter what the situation. But to help you get started, we're going to focus on natural disasters in this part.

Nature can be amazingly beautiful, but it can also be dangerous and deadly. Natural disasters are regular occurrences that threaten our property, our food sources, and even our lives.

It is vitally important to protect our families and our homes from these random acts of destruction. However, if you are prepared, you have a better chance of coming out the other side with minimal damage.

Safeguarding your home and family needs to happen before the disaster. Here are some of the most common natural disasters and what you can do to prepare.

Floods

Floods are some of the most common natural disasters in the United States. While floods are thought to occur only near large bodies of water, they can also take place near small creeks and streams.

Usually, you will have some warning regarding floods. They normally develop slowly over hours or days of heavy rainfall. But you still need to be prepared for flash floods. Roaring water and debris can cause massive damage to any property or person in its path.

There are many precautions you can take if you live in an area that is known to flood.

First, seal your home's foundation with a waterproof compound. You can also build floodwalls to lower the amount of water that seeps into your home.

Floods are some of the most common natural disasters in the United States.

In case of extreme flooding, if water gets into the house, take the following precautions. First, disconnect all electrical appliances and utilities from the source. Next, move to the highest level of your home. Finally, listen to a battery-powered radio for information and directions.

Do not attempt to drive through the flood. If you didn't get out before it began, hunkering down may be your best option.

Earthquakes

Unlike floods, earthquakes generally do not indicate that they are about to occur. They happen when the tectonic plates in the earth's crust suddenly shift, collide, or slide.

Depending on how strong the earthquake is, it can severely damage the surface of the earth—and the buildings, bridges, and roads on top of that surface. The damage can range from a mild shake that slightly rattles the windows up to an extreme displacement of the ground that demolishes buildings. In the most severe cases, thousands of people may perish, with thousands more injured.

If you live along a fault line, take these precautions.

Make sure that the foundation of your house is stable and that the house is bolted to the foundation. Many earthquake-prone areas have housing contractors that specialize in preparing homes for earthquakes. Check with your local licensing board for contractors, or use an internet search engine to find one that can help.

Secure heavy appliances to the floor, such as the water heater and stove. Securing these items is easy. But if you aren't good at handyman projects or DIY (Do-It-Yourself), plumbers and electricians can do this work for you.

During an earthquake, the injuries people experience are

usually caused by falling objects or objects becoming airborne. The best tactic is to "drop, cover, and hold on."

Drop down to the ground, then try to crawl under a table or desk. If there is no table or desk, crawl to the nearest interior wall. Get face down and cover your head and neck with your arms. Hold on until the shaking stops.

When the ground stops moving, turn off your water, gas, and electricity until you can assess the damage.

Hurricanes

Hurricanes are defined as the circular flow of winds that exceed 75 miles per hour. They form over tropical waters and move toward land. While islands in tropical waters have the highest risk, the coastal areas of main continents are also significantly affected. The damage becomes less intense as the hurricane moves more inland, though there is still a flood risk from heavy rain. The extreme winds carry debris and water into the air, causing damage and life-threatening situations. Hurricanes usually happen between June and November.

If you live in an area prone to hurricanes, you need to have an emergency kit and a weather radio with additional batteries. (See our checklist at the end of the book.)

Hurricane prediction has become commonplace, although the strength of the winds is hard to determine. If you are not evacuating, have a safe room that is away from the main walls. If there is a mandatory evacuation, please follow it and do not try to rough out the storm.

You can also fortify your home so it is less likely to be damaged by the extreme winds or flying objects. Contact a housing contractor in your area who specializes in home hurricane prepping.

This shorefront home was ruined by Hurricane Katrina.

Tornadoes

A tornado begins to form when a thunderstorm is unstable. When warm air hits cooler air, it may form a rotating tunnel that can touch land. The excessive winds can lift cars into the air, uproot trees, and send homes crashing to the ground. The winds can reach more than 250 miles per hour and become deadly if they pick up debris.

While tornadoes can occur anywhere, certain parts of the United States experience them more frequently. The Midwest is known for frequent and deadly tornadoes, and there is some evidence tornado activity is shifting east and south.

You can protect your home against the tornado winds by

fortifying doors and walls, adding shutters to the outside of windows, and ensuring that the trees on your property are healthy. A healthy tree is more likely to stay rooted and not have loose branches that turn into "flying missiles."

During the tornado, make sure that all of your windows are closed and retreat to the basement, or to a room in the interior of the house that has no windows. As with earthquakes, you should drop, cover, and hold on. Get underneath a heavy piece of furniture, like a table or desk, to protect yourself from falling debris. Keep water, food, and a first aid kit in the basement in case of a severe storm.

Natural disasters can uproot trees, causing property damage.

Hailstorms

Hailstorms aren't usually considered a natural disaster. However, they can be extremely destructive. Hailstorms cause an estimated one billion dollars' worth of property damage every year.

Hail forms during a storm when drops of rain freeze in the upper atmosphere. Typically, the hail is small and causes little to no damage. However, hail can become as big as softballs or larger. When this happens, it can break windows, damage cars, and injure people.

To protect your family and home against hail damage, keep up on maintenance of your house. A sturdy roof will not be as susceptible to damage.

During a hailstorm, make sure your car is in a garage, and all your children and pets are in the house.

Hailstorms can damage property and injure people.

If the hail is extremely large, cover the windows with curtains or blankets if you can, or at least stay away from any windows. If it breaks the glass in a window, the shattered pieces could launch inward.

Fortifying and Prepping Your Home against Natural Disasters

WHEN MOST PEOPLE THINK OF HUNKERING DOWN FOR DISASTER, they think of having emergency supplies, like water, food, first aid kits, and blankets. But your first concern should be your shelter. You need to make sure that your home is prepped and "hunker-ready" BEFORE disaster strikes.

And don't underestimate the emotional value of preparing your home. Living through a tornado, earthquake, wildfire, or flood is one of the most traumatic experiences a person can have. Add to this the heartbreak of seeing your home and belongings damaged or even destroyed, and it's no wonder people are looking for any way to prepare for the unexpected.

While home insurance protection is there to pick up the pieces after an unavoidable catastrophe happens, fortifying your home is a way of minimizing the overall damage that can occur.

Again, check with your local contractor's licensing board or use an internet search engine to find contractors who can help inspect and fortify your home.

To help make sure your shelter is prepped and ready, below is a list of some of the primary areas on which to focus.

Fortified Home Construction

When a natural disaster impacts an area or region, the social and financial costs of rebuilding homes and communities can be enormous. For these reasons, a nonprofit organization known as the Insurance Institute for Business & Home Safety (IBHS) has developed sets of building codes designed to help homeowners fortify their homes against natural disasters.

In most cities and counties, building code regulations provide a baseline guide for home and commercial buildings. Building a home to code ensures the basic overall structure is solid and sound.

The IBHS has also developed an enhanced set of guidelines known as a "code-plus" program that goes over and above what the local building codes require. In effect, these guidelines are designed to strengthen the areas in a home's construction most vulnerable to the impact of a natural disaster.

Roofing

In areas where tornadoes or hurricanes are likely, fortifying a home's roof can go a long way toward reducing overall damage. Even in cases where a roof remains intact after a catastrophe, a weakened roof covering opens up the possibility of water entry, which can damage and weaken a home's structure.

Ways to fortify a roof include ensuring the framing and covering can withstand the effects of high force winds, rain, and hail. This means the ends of the roof or gable framing should be braced back toward the interior portion of the roof to prevent winds from getting underneath. The roof deck portion that attaches to the frame and sits underneath the shingles should be at least 19/32 inches thick and firmly attached to the frame. Using thick, quality-grade shingle covering is also essential.

Placing a secondary water barrier or seal on top of the roof deck provides yet another layer of protection against potential water damage. This barrier is designed to remain intact in instances where storms blow shingles off the roof. For a full seal effect, it's also important to seal off the deck joints where the frame attaches to the deck. The IBHS recommends using a self-adhering, polymer-modified bitumen roofing tape for deck joint seals.

Load Path

A big part of your home's design has to do with how weight loads are distributed throughout the home's structure. The connections or bracings between the roof, walls, and different floors are designed to distribute weight from the top down evenly. When done correctly, your home's framework and structure will remain solid and intact. Load paths run from the rooftop to the lowest levels of the house.

Fortifying your home's load path involves ensuring the structures that make up the path are properly constructed. The roof's connection to the walls consists of strapping hardware—also known as hurricane straps—that joins rafters and trusses to underlying support walls. A solid support wall should be made of concrete block with vertical reinforcements or ties and horizontal beam reinforcements at the top of each wall section.

Ensuring a solid connection between your home's structure and its foundation requires wall bracings at four-foot intervals between foundation and flooring, and also where corners and wall openings exist. For exterior structures like carports and porches, anchor connections help to ensure these structures stay intact and connected to the main building.

Fortifying your home's load path may reduce damage during a natural disaster.

Windows and Doors

Local building codes require all windows and doors to meet certain impact and pressure resistance standards. Most code regulations equip home structures to withstand winds of 90 miles per hour, which is about the force of a weak tornado. Fortifying windows and doors against extreme disaster conditions involves reinforcing window designs and strengthening doorways.

Window reinforcements can be as simple as applying solar/safety film across glass surfaces. This prevents glass from blowing inside the house and injuring you or a family member. You can also replace existing window sets with impact-resistant glass or double-pane glass windows. Adding on permanent storm shutters can also help to reinforce vulnerable window openings.

Reinforcing doorways involves strengthening the connectors and bracings that hold a door in place. Doorways with three hinges as opposed to two provide a stronger connection to walls. Replacing deadbolt mechanisms with bolts that span at least one inch in length will maintain a stronger brace between the door's free-side and the wall.

Home Equipment

In addition to fortifying your home, there are a many essential home equipment items you might want to have on hand during and after the natural disaster.

Generator

A home generator can supply your home with power should you lose electricity. It will allow you to keep such essentials as heaters, air conditioners, lights, refrigerators, and freezers running during a power outage.

There are two basic types of home generators. Permanent, fixed generators, called standby generators, are designed to be installed permanently at your home. They are connected to the house wiring and are immediately ready to use when needed. Some even automatically start when the power drops, then stop when the power resumes.

This type of generator is expensive and should be installed by a licensed electrician, which adds to the expense. But they are generally more powerful and easier to use than our second type of generator, the portable generator.

Portable generators are more economical and can be stored when not in use. When needed, you must to roll it out of storage and fill with fuel, and run extension cords from the generator to the areas of your home that require power. Since portable generators have far less power than standby generators, you will need to decide which appliances to run or not run. You must also periodically fill it with fuel to keep it running.

A home generator can help supply your home with power should you lose electricity. Credit: CC BY-SA 3.0 courtesy of Gbleem.

Heater

You may also want to consider a space heater, especially if you live in a cold climate.

An electric space heater is easy to operate but will need a backup generator in a power outage.

Kerosene heaters are handy if you don't have a generator. Kerosene has a long shelf life, but be sure to store it safely in approved containers away from sunlight, make sure you use it in a well-ventilated area, and don't leave it unattended.

You can also use portable propane heaters in smaller areas. Once again, ventilation is crucial, and all components of your heater, such as the nozzles and hoses, must be compatible and tightly sealed.

No matter what type of heater you use, follow all the safety precautions that come with the instructions.

Other Tools

Depending on where you live, and on the type of disaster, you may also want to keep tools such as chainsaws and shovels on hand. Chainsaws are handy to help cut up fallen trees from your yard after a storm, and shovels are great for digging temporary drainage ditches to channel water away from the foundation or basement of your home before a storm hits.

The Myth of the 72-Hour Emergency Kit

MOST OFFICIALS AND EMERGENCY ORGANIZATIONS RECOMMEND that people put together "72-hour" emergency kits. These kits consist of 72 hours' worth of food, water, and emergency supplies for your family. The theory is that during a disaster, it may take up to three days for "help" to arrive.

This help might be in the form of government-sponsored relief, such as the US Federal Emergency Management Agency (FEMA), or it might be from the Red Cross, or other non-government disaster relief efforts, or perhaps merely restoration of standard utilities such as water and electricity after a disaster.

However, many preppers see a 72-hour kit as woefully inadequate for three reasons. One is that it can take much longer for disaster recovery to take place, the slow response to Hurricane Katrina a prime example. Second, in some situations, even with a quick response, disaster relief might be overwhelmed and not able to respond to everyone's needs.

The third reason is that there might be some disasters of the nonnatural kind where help won't be coming for a long time, such as economic collapse, martial law, or governmental collapse. Although we're focused primarily on natural disasters, we can't forget that these are possible, as well.

Therefore, a 72-hour kit isn't adequate for decent survival prepping.

At a minimum, your emergency kit should include 10 days of food, water, and emergency supplies. A 30-day supply would be better, 90 days even more so. Six months would be better still, while up to a year's worth of supplies would be ideal.

Of course, this depends on your financial resources and the storage space you have in your home. But what I often find when talking with new preppers is that the prospect of gathering a year's worth of supplies seems overwhelming. It's usually a mental barrier that prevents people from being adequately prepped.

So we're going to focus on helping you put together a 10-day supply of emergency supplies. We're doing that for two reasons. First, the 10-day supply is a good place to start. It is easy to put together that amount of food and emergency supplies without getting overwhelmed by all the details.

Second, it's far better than a mere 72-hour kit, and it will get you through many natural disasters without having to rely on immediate relief.

So look at this 10-day kit as your first step. Once you see how easy it is to put together, it will give you the confidence to build it into a larger kit. Then you can set a new goal—say, a 30-day kit. Just add more food, water, and supplies until you reach the 30-day level. Then you can set the next goal, a 90-day kit.

Keep working your way up, step-by-step, and before you know it, you'll be fully prepped.

But this all starts with that first step. Are you ready? Let's get started on your 10-day kit with the most essential items— water and food.

Water: Storage, Alternate Sources, and Purification

DURING AN EMERGENCY, AFTER SHELTER, WATER IS ONE OF THE most important considerations. You can survive days without food, but you will not survive as long without water.

How to Store Water for an Emergency

Storing water requires glass containers or food-grade plastic. These containers can be purchased from outdoor and hardware stores and come in sizes of one, three, or five gallons.

If you choose plastic containers, make sure that these containers are "BPA-Free." Bisphenol A (BPA) is an industrial chemical that can leach from the plastic into the water during storage.

In addition to specialized containers, a container that has previously held water or food would be acceptable for storing water. For example, two-liter soda bottles and milk jugs are an option. Stainless steel can also be used to store water if the water has not been treated with bleach, as the bleach will corrode the steel.

For storing large amounts of water for the family, some people use 55-gallon drums. These drums aren't as large as they might sound. Usually, they are only three feet tall and two feet in diameter. When they are empty, they weigh only about 25 pounds.

However, once they are full of water, they will be heavy, and you may have difficulty moving them around. But if you have space, 55-gallon drums are ideal for hunkering down.

You can also choose food-grade, High-Density Polyethylene (HDPE) containers. Once again, look for BPA-free containers. They should be thoroughly cleaned with hot water and soap and be rinsed with a solution containing one tablespoon of bleach per gallon of water. Stainless steel should be placed in boiling water for 10 minutes.

Storing water requires glass containers or food-grade plastic.

Clearly mark your drinking water, including the storage date, and store it in a dry and cool place that is not near sunlight or other forms of heat.

Water should also be stored away from pesticides, kerosene, and gasoline, as well as changed every six months to 12 months. It is also a good idea to have a gallon of water in the freezer to keep perishables cold until power restoration. When filling a water jug to freeze, don't fill it all the way and leave some space for the water to expand or the jug will crack.

How Much Water to Store

There are differing opinions on how much water to store. The minimum recommendation is one gallon of water per person, per day. But that's the bare minimum for relatively healthy adults in a mild climate.

Water storage amounts may vary based upon the person's physical condition, diet, and climate. Children, sick people, and nursing mothers will require more water. If you live in the desert, or in warmer or drier climates, you should double the daily amount per person.

An additional gallon or so of water per person may also be required per day for bathing, washing dishes, and hygiene.

To be fully prepped, we suggest three gallons of water per day, per person. So a family of four should store about 12 gallons of water per day. If you use two 55-gallon drums, that would be about a 10-day supply for the family.

How to Find Alternate Water Sources during an Emergency

In an emergency, there are several alternate water sources if commercial water is not available. Here are a few suggestions if you have not stored enough water to prepare for the natural disaster.

Drain Available Water from the Public Water Supply

Drain water from the plumbing system if the public water supply is still safe. A typical water heater holds 30 to 60 gallons of water and can be beneficial in an emergency. Before draining, the electricity or gas should be turned off, and allow the water heater to cool before draining to prevent scalding.

The first few gallons may contain rust or sediment. Drain the first few gallons and discard the water. When the cleaner water is obtained, add five to seven drops of chlorine bleach per gallon of water and let it sit for 30 minutes before consumption.

The water in your water heater can be used during an emergency. Credit: CC BY 2.0 courtesy of Brian Cantoni.

Outdoor Water Sources

Streams, lakes, rivers, natural springs, and ponds can be used if the water is first treated (see below). Do not consume flood water or water with odor or a dark color. Saltwater can be consumed if the water is distilled first (see below).

Swimming Pools

Pools are a source of backup water and can be used if the maintenance level is between three and five parts per million of free chlorine. Boil the water to five parts per million before drinking the water. Use the chlorine test kit that you use with your pool to test the boiled water and keep the pool covered until the water is needed.

How to Purify Questionable Water

If you are uncertain if the water you have is safe to drink, there are several ways to purify it.

Purify water by boiling, then adding standard household bleach. Credit: CC BY 2.0 courtesy of Mike Mozart.

Boil and Chlorinate the Water

Water can be purified with boiling and chlorination, with boiling times varying based upon the altitude. In general, a rolling boil for five to ten minutes is safe at sea level. Longer times may be required at higher altitudes.

After boiling, let the water cool first. Then add five to seven drops (which is approximately one-eighth of a teaspoon) of chlorine bleach to each gallon of water. Shake the solution and store in a dry and cool place for at least 30 minutes. If the water smells of chlorine, it will be safe to consume.

The bleach used should be standard household bleach with 8.25 percent sodium hypochlorite. The label should clearly state that the bleach is suitable for disinfection and sanitation. Avoid bleaches with scents, as they may not be safe to consume, as well as bleaches that say "color safe" or have added cleaning agents. The bleach should have been stored at room temperature and should be no more than one year old.

Filter and Chlorinate the Water

Purchase a filter at a sporting goods store that will remove parasites. Since filters will not eliminate all bacteria and viruses, add five to seven drops of chlorine bleach to each gallon of filtered water and wait 30 minutes before consumption.

Distill the Water

Distillation is the process of boiling water and then capturing the vapor when it condenses back to water, which will be free of impurities and salt.

A distilling flask along with a heat source such as a camp stove can make distilling much easier. You can purchase one online, from stores that sell chemistry supplies, and from some camping and outdoor stores. Just follow the instructions that come with the flask.

If you don't have a distilling flask, you can still perform the distillation process, although it is a bit more difficult and time-consuming. You will need a pot with a lid, a cup, and some string or rope to tie the cup to the lid. Place the lid on top of the cup and tie it to the lid and handle. The cup needs to be held securely in place, with a little space between the top of the cup and the lid. You may need to have a family member hold the lid and cup as you tie it on. The cup should be upright when the lid is placed back on the pot.

Fill the pot halfway with water and set boil. Place the lid on the pot, so that the cup is suspended above the water. As the water boils, the steam will hit the lid, condense into water, and drop into the cup. Use the water from the cup. Discard any water left in the pot, as it will contain the impurities left behind.

Note that distilling water is a time-consuming process. It should only be used if you can boil the water but do not have access to chlorine bleach. Boiling and chlorinating are much easier.

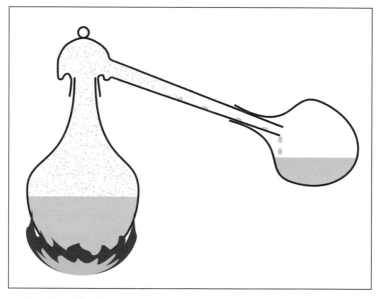

A distilling flask makes it easier to heat impure water and catch the pure vapor. Credit: CC BY-SA 3.0 courtesy of Urutseg, trengarasu, Gustavb, H Padleckas.

Food: Stocking Your Larder to Survive

WITH A LITTLE TIME AND COMMITMENT, YOU CAN STOCK UP YOUR food pantry or basement with a variety of healthy and nutritious foods that will help to sustain your family during a natural disaster and the aftermath of one.

If you are a busy person who works and cares for your family, you may think you don't have enough time on your hands to create and store foods. However, by setting aside just one day each month for preparations, you can take positive steps to provide for your family during unexpected crisis events.

Your Survival Larder

Your survival larder is the place where you'll keep your family's emergency food. This larder should be in an area that will most likely survive a natural disaster. If you have a basement, that may be the best place for you to put your larder. If you don't have a basement, a location along an interior wall near the inside of the house is probably the best bet.

You may be wondering if having an emergency larder is necessary. After all, you are in your home. Can't you just put your emergency food in your kitchen with the rest of your food?

Well, maybe. However, there might be cases where part of your home becomes unusable during a natural disaster. You might not be able to get access to your kitchen, while the rest of your house is useable. It may be wise to have two or three emergency larders spread around your home just in case.

More important, having your emergency food in separate larders allows you to inspect it periodically to check the dates to make sure it is still good.

If you are putting all of your emergency supplies together in one location such as a basement, it is crucial that you have separate shelving units for chemical cleaning and personal items to keep them away from the food items you will store to ensure toxins are not spilled into the food.

Stocking Your Larder

Any foods that have a long shelf life and don't require refrigeration are good candidates for stocking your larder. Most canned goods in your local grocery store fit this bill. Canned foods with high-liquid ratios will also reduce the need for drinking water. Canned meats, soups, chili, beans, and stews can form the basis of your emergency meals. These items are usually fully cooked, so if you don't have any way to heat these items, you can consume them directly from the can. Just make sure you have a can opener stored with your emergency supplies.

You can also add items like canned fruits and vegetables to your storage area for additional nutrients and variety. In addition, soup, fruit juices, and drinks that come in aseptic, "juice box" style packaging often have long shelf lives, as well. You can also find "canned" foods (that is, food preserved in an air-tight glass jar) such as fruits and pickled vegetables. However, glass

Stock your larder with foods that have a long shelf life and don't require refrigeration.

jars are breakable, so it would be best to stick with items in metal cans.

Beyond canned and aseptic items, many camping and outdoor stores offer a wide selection of MRE ("Meals Ready to Eat") packages, including some that are self-heating. Self-heating packages are convenient in an emergency, especially when it isn't safe to use your camp stove or light a fire. You can also find dehydrated camping meals that may require adding water and heat.

Additional Food Suggestions

Peanut butter or other nut butters are great items to store in your emergency storage room. Peanut butter provides healthy fats and protein, as well as adequate amounts of nutrition when paired with fruit or canned vegetables.

Snack bars made of granola, protein, or fruit work well, as do dry cereals or ready-to-eat granola. Dried fruit that is similar to the fresh fruit favorites your family enjoys is a good option, and shelled nuts are a good source of nutrition. Many of these items can be bought in bulk. Just make sure you store them in airtight containers to keep them fresh.

Since bread usually has a poor shelf life, crackers can substitute and will last longer. In addition, canned, pasteurized milk can be a substitute for fresh milk.

You may also want to include vitamins and other dietary supplements your family needs. Don't forget infant foods, as well as comfort foods such as candy and other favorites. During

Bulk foods are an inexpensive way to stock your larder.

an emergency, you'd be surprised how welcome a comfort food is to help keep your spirits up.

Cooking and Eating during an Emergency

One of the best ways to be prepared for a natural disaster is to ensure you have all the necessary cooking items stored in your emergency storage room. A small charcoal grill will allow you to cook outside the home if electricity is not available. Be sure to stock up on several bags of charcoal, lighter fluid, spatulas, and grill cleaner. It is also a smart idea to store away a large supply of paper towels, paper plates, and utensils. If both water and electricity are out, disposable items are going to be lifesavers.

If you use a charcoal grill, it is imperative you only use it outside. As an alternative, you can also get a small propane

Add a small camping stove or hot plate to your emergency supplies.

stove for indoor use. Make sure to have backup propane cylinders.

Because you never know in advance if you will have electricity available, you will want to store an electric hot plate and a small pot or two in your storage room. Canned meats, vegetables, and fruits, however, do not need to be heated to provide sustenance.

As you are building up the items in your storage room for emergency situations, use the checklist at the back of this book. You'll find that we recommend storing utensils, plastic drinking cups, trash bags, basic dish soap, hand soap, hand sanitizer, and a can opener. Add to the list any items that will help make your cooking and food preparation go more smoothly.

Hygiene: The Biggest Threat to Your Hunkering-Down Health and Safety

WHEN PREPARING FOR A DISASTER, MANY PEOPLE THINK ABOUT things like stockpiling food and batteries. However, they do not think about things like hygiene and sanitation.

Realistically, the threats posed by poor hygiene and sanitation are more dire than the risk of starvation, and if you find yourself in a disaster situation, it is essential that you know how to prevent infection and the spread of disease. Make sure that you are acquainted with these important tips to keep yourself and your family safe.

Get Rid of Contaminated Food

The food that you eat during an emergency situation must be uncontaminated, as food poisoning can pose a serious risk.

If your food has come in contact with storm water or flood water, throw it out. Similarly, throw out any perishable food if it has been in your refrigerator for longer than four hours after the power has gone out.

The phrase to always keep in mind is "When in doubt,

throw it out." Use your best judgment. If the food has a strange color, texture, or odor, throw it away.

Boil Your Water

Water can carry many diseases if it is not treated.

We covered how to purify water in an earlier chapter, but just a reminder: in most cases, water can be rendered harmless and drinkable through bringing it to a boil, filtering, or adding a disinfectant such as chlorine bleach before drinking. It is important to remember that boiling water does not work for all situations. If toxic chemicals, gasoline, or oil have contaminated the water, do not drink it.

Human Waste

Human waste is a serious issue during an emergency. The most important priority is to find a way to dispose of it that does not create a situation where food or food preparation surfaces are affected.

For example, in situations where the water is not running, a garbage bag can be slid over the toilet bowl, creating a reservoir for the waste that can be sealed when it is not in use and disposed of later on. Chemicals like quicklime will neutralize the waste and keep the odor down.

Similarly, you can purchase a "honey bucket"—a specially designed bucket for capturing and storing human waste. A bucket of this sort is easily sealed and neutralized with baking soda.

Be smart about your waste; if you have a latrine or a portable toilet on hand, locate it at least 100 feet away from your food prep areas.

A "honey bucket" is specially designed for capturing and storing human waste. Credit: CC BY-SA 2.0 courtesy of Alan Sim.

Wash Your Hands

In an emergency situation, germs can spread very quickly via skin-to-skin contact. To minimize the effect of germs, keep your hands clean by washing them with clean water and soap.

Most people wash their hands thoughtlessly, but during an emergency, you'll want to take extra care. Rub a wet lather of soap between your hands for at least 20 seconds, taking care to clean under your fingernails and on the backs of your hands, and then rinse them off completely. This can help prevent the spread of illness.

If clean water is scarce, use alcohol-based wipes to keep your hands free and clear of germs and disease.

Wound Care

Some small wounds can be taken care of at home during an emergency situation.

We'll discuss first aid in more detail in the next chapter, but here are the basics: always using clean hands and water, make sure to clean the wound and then apply a small amount of antibacterial cream before covering it with a bandage. Covering a wound will keep it from getting infected as it heals.

Rinse it out with soap and water at least once a day to further prevent the chances of infection. Signs that more serious care is needed include swelling, seeping, or redness. If a wound feels warm to the touch, it is also a sign that you may need further medical attention.

Infant Care

Infants and very young children are often the most vulnerable people during an emergency situation. If you have a child who is breastfeeding, he or she should continue to breastfeed if at all possible. If the child in question is on a formula solution that requires water, make sure that you only prepare the formula with clean water. Make sure that all of the infant's bottles and feeding equipment are sanitized with hot water after every use.

Canned Food Concerns

Many people stockpile canned foods for emergencies, but it is also important to remember that canned foods can also be contaminated. For example, if the can is bulging, there is a buildup of gas inside, meaning the food is inedible and should be thrown away.

Similarly, if the can has been sitting in contaminated water of any sort, it needs to be disinfected. Check the label to see the contents and expiration date. Remove the label and dip the can into a mixture of five gallons of water and one cup of bleach. Rinse the can off, and then use a permanent marker to relabel the contents and expiration date.

Food Contact Surfaces

A food contact surface is any surface used in food preparation. In most cases, this means cutting boards and countertops. Any surface that you suspect has been contaminated should be washed with soap and clean water and then rinsed. After that, it can be sanitized with a solution made from about one teaspoon of bleach and a gallon of clean water. Allow the surface to air-dry for the best results.

Some Things Cannot Be Made Safe

During a disaster, particularly one that involves water, there will be some things that cannot be kept safe.

For example, wooden cutting boards and wooden cooking utensils should likely be tossed. Wood is porous, and bacteria can grow in very small cracks where scrubbing cannot reach.

On top of that, you should also throw out any pacifiers or bottle nipples that have come into contact with contaminated water. If you are not sure if something is contaminated, it's always better to be safe than sorry. When in doubt, throw it out.

During an emergency, make sure that you are thoroughly prepared to deal with hygiene and sanitation issues. This can significantly improve your experience of hunkering down, avoiding much stress at a difficult time.

Your First Aid Kit: When Medical Help Isn't Available

Being prepared for a natural disaster is a must, especially if you live in areas that are prone to such events. A first aid kit is a necessity and should be well marked and fully stocked at all times.

Assembling Your FIrst Aid Kit

The most critical item in your first aid kit? A printed first aid booklet.

Unless you have had some first aid training, it's always a good idea to have a booklet that lists different first aid techniques. Even if you have had minimal training, something to refer to in times of high stress can be comforting. Go to your local bookstore to find one or search your online bookstore for "first aid booklet."

Besides a first aid booklet, other items you need to include are:

- Sterile gauze, both 2x2 and 4x4 sizes
- Medical tape—either paper, silk, or plastic

A well-stocked first aid kit is a necessity for survival prepping.

- Adhesive bandages in multiple sizes
- Several rolls of three- or four-inch self-adherent elastic wrap
- Compression wraps—at least two four-inch wraps
- Several antiseptic wipes
- Antibacterial liquid soap
- Triple antibiotic ointment—preferably with lidocaine
- One bottle of peroxide
- A tube of anti-itch cream
- One bottle of chewable aspirin tablets commonly referred to as baby aspirin
- Tweezers

- Bandage scissors
- A few large safety pins
- Medical-grade cold compresses
- Calamine lotion
- Cotton balls
- One bottle of alcohol or a box of alcohol wipes
- Thermometer
- Latex gloves—you can use polyurethane or vinyl if you have a latex allergy
- A small flashlight with batteries
- A small box of diphenhydramine/antihistamine allergy tablets
- Tongue depressors
- Several bottles of water
- Over-the-counter NSAID medications (ibuprofen) and other pain relievers

Make sure to check your first aid kit on a regular basis and replace items that have been used or are out of date. All of these can be found at your local pharmacy, although some products may be behind the counter. If you are unable to find what you need, ask the pharmacist.

First Aid Skills and Techniques
Below are some of the most common ailments, as well as ways to treat them using items from your newly stocked first aid kit.

Please also check your first aid booklet for additional treatment options.

Anaphylaxis
This is the most severe form of allergic reaction. People who

suffer from anaphylaxis can go from being completely fine one minute to not breathing the next.

These people will need professional medical assistance immediately. However, there are a few things you can do to assist the person suffering from anaphylaxis.

First, call for emergency assistance, if phone lines are open and someone hasn't already done so.

As the person with anaphylaxis often knows they have life-threatening allergies, he or she sometimes will carry an epinephrine auto-injector, also known as an "EpiPen." Ask the person if he or she has one or, if they are unconscious, search through his or her pockets for one. If a member of your family has allergies, make sure you store additional EpiPens in your first aid kit.

Administer the injection immediately and assist the person into a lying position to avoid injury if he or she loses consciousness. Cover them with a light blanket or sweatshirt if possible. If they have tight clothing around the neck, loosen the clothing. Do not give him or her anything to drink! If they stop breathing, begin CPR and continue until someone more qualified arrives.

Bruises

Bruises can occur virtually anywhere on the body, especially when a person is hit by debris in a natural disaster. When surface blood vessels are broken, it allows blood to flow into the different layers of skin. Small bruises may not need treatment, but larger bruises, especially those where the point of impact is swollen, will need cold compresses applied several times a day. Over-the-counter NSAID medications like ibuprofen will help with pain and inflammation of the bruised area.

Abrasions

An abrasion is a scrape on the surface of the skin. It is not very deep and typically stops bleeding very quickly. It can be taken care of very quickly with an antiseptic wipe, adhesive bandages, and antibiotic ointment. Make sure you apply multi-use antibiotic ointment to the fresh adhesive bandage, rather than directly on the abrasion, so you aren't touching the tip of the tube with contaminated flesh or blood.

Lacerations

A laceration is a deep cut that often requires sutures or stitches. In an emergency situation when medical assistance is not readily available, there are several steps you can take to slow the bleeding and prevent infection.

Wipe the area with an antiseptic wipe or pour hydrogen peroxide over the wound and wipe it clean with sterile, 4x4 gauze. Apply pressure to the laceration to slow the bleeding. If necessary, cover the wound with several pieces of sterile gauze and wrap tightly with a self-adherent elastic wrap from your kit. If it's going to be a long time before medical treatment can be sought, periodically remove the pressure once in a while, especially if it's wrapped so tightly that you lose feeling in the area below the laceration.

Dislocations and Fractures

When an arm becomes dislocated, one shoulder will hang lower than the other. It's also possible to dislocate hips, thumbs, and elbows. If you suspect a dislocation, do not attempt to correct the problem on your own. Apply a cold compress to the area and immobilize it immediately. If the shoulder or elbow is suspected, wrap the affected limb tightly to the body with a compression wrap. Ibuprofen can help to minimize pain and associated swelling.

Fractures are broken bones. These injuries will also require immobilization. Use a tongue depressor and self-adherent elastic wrap or tape to immobilize fingers and wrists. When arms or legs are involved, you can use a baseball bat, broom, or mop handle, or anything else that's straight and long enough to immobilize the affected limb completely. Use Ibuprofen to decrease pain and swelling.

Puncture Wounds

If a person is impaled with an object, use a compression wrap to prevent the object from moving while it's inside the body. DO NOT remove the object, regardless of whether the person is conscious or unconscious.

CPR

It's always a good idea to have every member of the family become familiar with basic cardiopulmonary resuscitation (CPR) skills. These classes are normally offered at many different locations, including community college campuses, local recreation centers, Red Cross locations, and even in some churches and other organizations. Practice CPR as a family at least once a month, so it's familiar to everyone in case of an emergency.

Communications: Improving Your Situational Awareness

PROPER COMMUNICATION EQUIPMENT IS ESSENTIAL IN SURVIVING any disaster. You need to be aware of how the situation is developing in your area. You may also need to send messages and signals to get help and supplies. The following gear can help you stay abreast of news and communicate during natural disasters.

Landline Phones

A landline phone is one of the easiest communication devices to use during emergencies. Any member of the family who knows how to make a phone call can easily dial emergency numbers to inquire about the current nature and severity of the situation. Home phones are also accessible and ready for use at any time. You can contact neighbors, friends, and family to stay updated or to ask for help.

However, natural disasters can often damage phone lines and leave you with a landline phone that doesn't work. They can also cause damage to phone company offices, and this could cut off landline phone service. Finally, the sheer amount of people using the phone system during a disaster can prevent making calls.

To make sure you can fully use your landline, we recommend that you have at least one corded, nonelectric phone at home to use. The modern cordless phones may not charge properly during a power outage.

Mobile Phones

Almost everyone owns a cell phone these days. They are accessible and easy to use. They come in handy during natural disasters because they don't require physical phone lines. You also have the advantage of having emergency numbers stored in your cell phone. Being stuck in difficult situations can be much easier with a handy communication device.

Although a cell phone is a good way of communicating with other people, it also has its own disadvantages. Network providers in your area may have also been damaged by the disaster. This often causes phone service and signals to be irregular and even cut off. Phone networks may also experience congestion because a lot of people will use their mobile phones to communicate or get help. This will make it difficult for you to get through on the line or send text messages.

A cell phone's battery also lasts for only a few hours at the most. These phones need constant recharging. Because most natural disasters cause power outages, you will not be able to charge your phone, which is a major inconvenience if a mobile phone is the only communication device you have during an extended power outage. However, you can prepare by having an external or extra battery that is fully charged and ready for use. You might also want to have on hand a solar cell phone charger. If you conserve power by turning the phone off, you may miss incoming calls and news.

An alternative is a satellite phone, which will increase the chances of having a signal. Satellite phones are very similar to cell phones and just as easy to operate. While more expensive than standard cell phones, satellite service tends to be less affected by natural disasters than cell phones.

Note: Many people today no longer know the phone numbers of their extended family and friends, often relying on the contact list stored in their cell phone. However, if your cell phone loses power and you can't recharge it, you won't be able to access your contact list. So make sure you have a written or printed list of all your emergency contact numbers.

Broadcast Radio

Radios are a traditional way of sending messages to listeners during disasters. You can always stay updated about the hazards and safety measures with these devices. They are affordable and accessible, available for purchase online and in local shops at reasonable prices depending on the model.

Radios can either use electricity or batteries. Electrically powered radios are not practical during natural disasters, as you will have power outages most of the time. Battery-powered radios are ideal, and you can easily change the batteries once your radio runs out of power.

However, you will have to prepare extra batteries and refresh your stock, as they have expiration dates. Proper storage is also needed because they easily deteriorate with heat and moisture.

Another efficient option is to purchase solar-powered radios that don't require electricity or batteries and easily

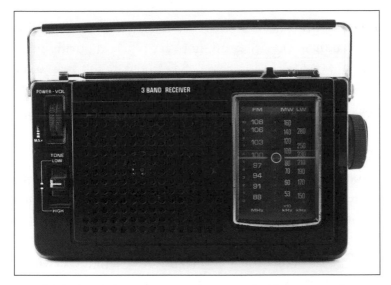

An old-fashioned transistor radio is a reliable means of staying informed during a disaster.

charge with sunlight. The downside to using solar radios is that they do not work at night, but you can also find hand-cranked transistor radios that you can power yourself.

In addition to the standard transistor radio, you may also want to consider having an NOAA Weather Alert Radio that picks up broadcasts directly from the US National Weather Service office. This office broadcasts around the clock, giving you the latest weather information for your area.

Broadcast Television

Televisions are also a good way of getting information. You can keep an eye on the progress and safety tips from private and public offices. Television stations are usually updated during natural disasters, as they contribute to the fast distribution of public knowledge. They typically work simultaneously with radio stations to inform the public about current news.

Although televisions provide viewers with current information about events, they are not very efficient during natural disasters. Most television sets need electricity to work, so they will be useless during outages. You need to have a backup generator if you prefer to watch the news on television.

Two-Meter Amateur Band Ham Radio

One common helpful device for any natural disaster is a two-meter amateur band ham radio, which allows amateur radio operators to stay in touch in challenging places or situations with the use of a repeater.

This radio set consists of a transmitter and a receiver that can contact other radio operators from 20 to 50 miles away, depending on if there are any working repeaters in the area. You can communicate with other radio operators using the same frequency. These ham radios are also built for heavy-duty use.

Although ham radios are often seen in survival kits, they require specific knowledge and expertise. In the US, you will also need a ham radio license issued by the FCC (Federal Communications Commission), which requires study plus a written exam. You also need to prepare spare batteries for these radios or have a backup generator ready for the emergency.

Citizens Band Radio

Having a citizens band radio, known as CB radio, can also be helpful in an emergency. CB radio has a much shorter range than ham radio, generally between one to five miles, and there are only 40 authorized channels shared among all CB radio users.

However, there are no licensing requirements to operate a CB radio within the United States. In addition, it's much easier to learn how to operate than a ham radio.

Once again, power is a consideration, so spare batteries or a backup generator may be necessary.

Walkie-Talkies

Walkie-talkies are handheld, two-way radios. They are much easier to use than ham or CB radios, but they have very limited ranges and are used for person-to-person communications. If you have neighbors or relatives who live physically close to you, these devices can help you maintain contact during an emergency.

Walkie-talkies are easy to use for limited-range communication.

There are two types of walkie-talkies in the United States. The range of an FRS (Family Radio Service) walkie-talkie, depending on obstructions, may be anywhere from one-third mile (half a kilometer) to one mile (or one and a half kilometers). So these are best suited for communicating with neighbors.

On the positive side, though, FRS walkie-talkies do not require licensing through the government and are relatively inexpensive.

GMRS (General Mobile Radio Service) walkie-talkies have a slightly larger range, up to two miles or three kilometers depending on obstructions. You can also add further range of up to five miles or eight kilometers with a higher antenna.

In the US, GMRS walkie-talkies require a license from the Federal Communication Commission (FCC). However, the licensing procedure is simple and does not require an examination or any specialized knowledge.

Once again, make sure you have spare power sources to keep your walkie-talkies working during an emergency.

Children: Removing the Fear of Hunkering Down

Infants

If you have infants, make sure you include all the usual daily care items in your emergency supplies, including diapers, baby wipes, infant formulas, and any medicine they may be taking. Make sure you store enough water for the formulas as well as for bathing your child.

Toddlers and School-Age Children

If you have small children, you want to involve them in your preparedness planning as much as possible for three reasons.

First of all, you want to make sure they are physically safe. Your children need to know what to do during an emergency to protect themselves. The second reason is that by involving them with the preparation plans, it helps ease their fears about emergency situations and builds their self-confidence.

Moreover, the third reason, and perhaps the most important, is that it increases the bond you have with your children and helps them build their trust in you. The family that prepares together not only stays safe together, but they create a common bond that improves family relationships.

Discuss Possible Emergencies with the Family

When you are planning for emergencies, you should involve the whole family. Start a family meeting and talk about the natural disasters that might occur in your local area. Ask for suggestions for plans that will keep the family safe during and after the emergency.

Involve your children with creating the plan. By getting your children involved in the process, you will ensure they understand the appropriate actions based on the situation. It also shows that parents value the opinions of children and are prepared to listen to suggestions, helping to build the teamwork that will be necessary in an emergency.

The discussion should always consider age-appropriate information for your children. Focus the discussion on planning options and working around the situation at home. While you might not be able to get to a school, daycare, or other location when children are out of the house, you should have a plan when they are at home. Suggest that older children help the younger family members if parents are not home, get hurt, or are not in the same room at the time of the emergency.

Emergency Supplies

So far in this book, we've already covered most of the basics about what to include in your emergency supplies for the whole family.

However, beyond the basics, when children are very young, you should also keep toys, books, and other entertaining diversions with your emergency supplies. You'll also want to include favorite pillows, blankets, or clothing. During an emergency, these items can reduce the tension and worries of your children. Have your children decide what they would like to keep in the emergency supplies, which will help them feel more a part of the preparedness planning.

Also, as you gather the supplies for the family, show your children where the items are located and explain when to use the emergency supplies. Teach them how to use the basic emergency items that are appropriate for their age. This not only helps them be prepared, but it also provide a level of protection in case you become injured during the emergency.

Add comfort items and diversions for your kids to your emergency supplies.

Teach Children Emergency Numbers

While some natural disasters might knock out the power or prevent calls, your children should still know the appropriate emergency numbers. Teach your children to dial 9-1-1 from a young age and provide a number to reach appropriate adults in case children become separated during the chaos of a natural disaster.

Practice with Your Children

The only way to ensure the family is fully prepared for the worst is through practice. Take time to practice different emergency situations and applying the plan to the situation. For example, if you are planning for the possibility of tornadoes, then you should focus on moving the family into the basement or getting underground.

Practice makes it easier to spot problems with the plan and discuss solutions at the next family meeting. If you are not practicing, then the possibility of something going wrong during a natural disaster is much higher.

If you have infant children, then it is doubly important to practice for different emergencies. Determining who will be responsible for getting the infant to safety will prevent a tragedy if a natural disaster strikes the area.

Get Your Children's School Involved

When you are planning for a natural disaster, you need to recognize that the family might not be at home during the event. Getting your children's school involved in disaster preparedness will help you determine the best solution when children are not at home.

Talk to their school about policies regarding local disasters. For example, if the area is prone to earthquakes, then you should ask about earthquake drills and getting in contact with children after the event. Finding out how their school handles disasters will help you determine the options available to help get children out of school after a disaster.

Test Children Regularly

After ensuring your children understand the emergency plans, you should test them on a regular basis. Ask children questions to determine if they remember the plan and test their knowledge about the location of emergency supplies.

Learn and Teach First Aid

While the plan and practice are important, you also want to learn first aid and teach children the basics in case injuries occur during an emergency. Children need to know where the first aid kit is located, the basics of cleaning cuts, and the different types of bandages that are appropriate for the size of the cut.

Earthquakes, hurricanes, hail storms, tornadoes, and other natural disasters can result in injuries. By preparing for the possibility of an injury, you will help keep the whole family safe from tragedy.

There are online resources that can help you create an emergency plan for your children. This page is from a government website: www.fema.gov/media-library/assets/documents/34330.

Pets: Hunkering Down with Our Furry Family Members

YOUR PETS WILL BE HUNKERING DOWN WITH YOU, SO YOU NEED to consider your pets' needs when it comes to prepping for your family's safety and survival.

Create a Pet Emergency Kit

Much like the emergency supplies you are gathering for yourself and your children, it is critical to have the essentials gathered to keep your pets safe and happy. Some items you will want to consider for a pet emergency kit include:

Food and Water

Perhaps the two most essential parts of any kit are food and water. Have at least the same amount of food and water for your pets as you do for yourself. Keep both in a safe, airtight container.

Medicine

If your pets take any medication, having several extra days' worth of pills stored in a safe, airtight container is also a good idea.

Collar with ID

Though dogs and cats should always be wearing their collars with ID and rabies tags at all times, make it a priority to know exactly where these items are. Keep a copy of this information in the emergency kit, as well.

Pet Carrier

During a disaster, even if you are hunkering down rather than evacuating, have a pet carrier handy. You may wish to keep your pets safe at night and at other times by placing them in the carrier.

A crate or carrier is a smart way to keep your pet safe when hunkering down. Courtesy of US Air Force.

First Aid Kit

Natural disasters can lead to minor pet injuries, so having a first aid kit to treat these injuries can help expedite your pets' healing. Speak with your veterinarian to learn what supplies to include with this kit. Usually, your kit should contain cotton bandage rolls, tape, scissors, flea and tick prevention, gloves, a pet first aid book, antibiotic ointment, and isopropyl alcohol and saline solution.

Sanitation

When appropriate, add litter, newspapers, trash bags, and bleach to your prepper supplies. The first few items should handle taking care of your pets' waste, and the bleach serves as

Favorite toys or beds can reduce stress for your pets.

a disinfectant for water. For every gallon of water, thoroughly stirring in eight drops of bleach and letting it sit for half an hour is sufficient to purify water. Ensure this is standard bleach, not color-safe or scented bleach.

Familiar items

Finally, though it is not inherently required to survive a disaster, having favorite toys or treats can reduce the stress your pets experience. Even a favorite bed will ensure that your pets remain calm and stress-free despite the disaster that occurs.

During and after a Disaster

If a natural disaster is about to occur, immediately bring your pets inside. The safest place for pets and humans alike is inside a home away from windows and other objects that can fly off a shelf and harm someone. Many pets have natural instincts about sudden changes in weather that cause them to act irrationally. Bringing them inside will help prevent them from running away.

Separate dogs, cats, and small pets. Even if your pets all usually get along with one another, a natural disaster can cause your pets stress that promotes irrational behavior. Small pets, such as hamsters, are especially susceptible to harm if a larger pet starts to act irrationally.

Keep a close eye on your pets' behavior. Since disasters can significantly stress out a pet, a normally quiet pet can become aggressive, so make sure to watch them closely while ensuring they have enough food and water.

Keep your pets on a leash whenever going outside for a few days after a disaster. Even if your pets usually run free in the backyard or neighborhood, disasters can alter familiar smells and landmarks, which can confuse a pet.

The Single Most Important Thing You Can Do to Ensure Your Family's Safety

AT THE END OF THIS BOOK, YOU'LL FIND CHECKLISTS THAT WILL help you get all of your supplies together. But supplies alone aren't enough.

What is the most important thing you can do to improve your survival and safety should you ever need to hunker down?

It is to PRACTICE your plan.

Once you have your emergency supplies, get together with your family and pick a day, or at least a few hours, to do a trial run.

Just as I suggested in the introduction, take a day or an afternoon and shut off all your utilities in your home. Shut off your water, gas, and electricity. Switch off the phones, the internet, and the cable. Stay in your house, right where you are, and have no contact with the outside world.

Use your emergency supplies and go through the next few hours. Cook and eat a meal from your supplies. Practice going to the bathroom and bathing. Try out your communications equipment. Go through your first aid booklet and check your first aid supplies. Spend time with your children and pets as you go through this trial run.

After the trial is over, remember to replenish the supplies you used during the trial.

These few hours will be the BEST investment you can make in your family's safety. At the end of those few hours, you'll know what worked, what didn't work, what you've forgotten, and what you need to know.

Most important, this trial will give you confidence. You'll know with certainty that you and your family are prepared to hunker down during an emergency.

You'll be amazed at the peace of mind this will give you, knowing you've prepared your family to be safe and secure, no matter what happens.

Practice your survival plan. Courtesy of US National Archives and FEMA.

PART 2

Get Out Of Dodge! Prepping to Leave Your Home and Bug Out during a Disaster

Hunkering Down vs. Bugging Out

BUGGING OUT IS THE OPPOSITE OF HUNKERING DOWN. IT'S ALL about making sure you have enough supplies and emergency gear ready to take with you if you need to evacuate your home and "get out of Dodge."

Visit any of the online prepper forums (there are quite a few these days), and you'll see preppers debating the merits of hunkering down versus bugging out. Some have only hunkering down plans, while others have only bug-out or evacuation plans. You'll find lots of debates and arguments about which of these two plans is better.

However, it's wrong to think of bugging out vs. hunkering down as an either/or choice. The best approach is to be prepared for both scenarios.

There is no one right answer to the question of whether to stay or to go because disaster scenarios are by their very nature unpredictable.

Disasters come in many forms, making it difficult to choose which scenario will make you best prepared. For example, if a hurricane stronger than a Category 1 is heading straight for your city or town, evacuation is best. Sometimes there are mandatory evacuations, and if you don't follow those instructions, you will have to wait until the storm has passed before you could count on any rescue. In a different scenario, if there is a tidal wave warning, you should also leave. So the hallmark of a successful survivor is adaptability. It is by being flexible, by being willing to adapt to a particular situation, that you will ensure the best possible chance of survival.

Start with Your Hunker-Down Plan

If you are brand new to prepping, I would suggest you start with the "hunker-down" plan we described in the first part of this book.

Putting together emergency supplies in your home is something you can do more easily and quickly than a bug-out plan. And because most people feel more secure and comfortable in their own home, it is best to keep supplies on hand that allow them to stay at home as long as possible.

But once you have your hunker-down plan in place, you should start focusing on your GOOD ("Get Out Of Dodge") bug-out plan. Then, once you have both methods down, you'll have a choice when disaster strikes.

A Disaster Strikes—Do We Stay or Do We Go?

Let's say that a disaster does strike, and you have both your hunker-down plan and your bug-out plan. Which should you use? Do you stay in your home or do you bug out?

I know there are many sides to this debate. Just look at the internet forums I mentioned above. But I'm of the opinion that if staying home is safe, it is probably best to stay at home for as long as possible.

Especially if you have a family, morale plays an enormous part in their mental well-being during a calamity. Home represents safety and security, two vital aspects of survival.

Even with the best of bug-out plans, your home contains more supplies than you can carry in a backpack or even load into a car. Rather than leave food, water, fuel, and tools behind, it is best to stay and use them for as long as possible, rather than attempt to carry them to some other location that may not be as secure.

A person's home can also be defended more readily than an unfamiliar or open location. Most people are aware of who their neighbors are and may have made friends who live nearby. Such a situation is far more desirable than the prospect of leaving home and being forced to find a place that is secure, possibly in an unknown location among strangers.

But when events transpire, or environmental conditions degrade to the point where it is no longer feasible or possible to remain at home, you should make the decision to leave sooner rather than later.

Whatever the unfortunate calamity that leads you to consider leaving your home, you should ensure you remain as informed as possible about the nature of your situation.

Most preppers have a distrust of government officials. But if officials are urging people to evacuate because of a fire, hurricane, or other natural disasters, I think you can trust their advice. There is simply no reason to stay at home if officials are expecting 15 feet of storm water to surge into an area. If, on the other hand, the government breaks down and there is no rule of law, you will need to decide for yourself when it is best to leave home.

Bug-Out Bags and Vehicle Kits

THE BASIS FOR ANY GOOD ("GET OUT OF DODGE") PLAN IS your bug-out bag. This is a bag with the emergency supplies you need to take with you to survive. Each member of your family will need a bug-out bag, with both their personal items and their "share of the load" the family will take with them. Young children should also have their own bug-out bag, even if they can't carry as much as the adults do.

And of course, if you are single, your bug-out bag will have to have everything you need, since you may not have family members or friends to share the load.

Two Bug-Out Bags

You may need two bug-out bags. One will have supplies if you need to bug out on foot or by bike. The other will have supplies if you can bug out by automobile.

The walking bug-out bag should be a high-quality backpack that is filled with necessary supplies. The bag will allow you to carry some food and water at the start but may also contain supplies for searching for food, filtering water, defending yourself, and sleeping outside under most conditions. Since this bag may need to be carried on your back for long distances, you'll need to limit it to only essentials.

The "vehicle kit" is like a bug-out bag, but stored in your car, truck, or RV. It can be a totally separate store of supplies, or it can have supplies that supplement a walking bug-out bag.

I like to have all my basic supplies in a walking bug-out bag, plus additional/extended supplies in a vehicle kit that I leave in my car. If I need to get out of Dodge and can do so by car, I can grab my "walking" bug-out bag and toss it in the car, so I have the combined supplies of both bags at my disposal. And should something happen during the journey that forces me to abandon the car, I can easily grab the bug-out bag and be on my way.

While I recommend spending the money to get a high-quality backpack, you don't need to spend a lot of money to stock it. You can get many of the products and resources for the bug-out bag for discounted prices if you shop smart. Keep your eye out for sales and buy essentials such as food, first aid materials, and nonperishables when they are on discount.

Selecting and Outfitting a Bug-Out Bag

The best way to select your bug-out bag is to imagine you are going on a multiday or extended camping and hiking trip.

The type of bag you choose will, of course, depend on the terrain in your area and in your bug-out location. In general, you will need more room for supplies for a longer trip to your bug-out location, for more difficult terrain, and for more difficult weather conditions such as extreme heat or extreme cold.

Your walking bug-out bag should be a high-quality backpack matched to the terrain.

Choose the bag for the worst conditions you'll face, not for the best or average conditions.

Backpacks are usually sold by "capacity" in either cubic inches or liters. Multiday packs are generally 60 to 80 liters or between 3,000 to 5,000 cubic inches. These backpacks are good for two-to-five-day trips. That should be considered the minimum for your bug-out bag to get you to your bug-out destination where you may have additional supplies.

If you have to travel longer, or if you don't have a cache of supplies at your bug-out location, an extended-trip backpack might be a better choice. These are greater than 80 liters or 5,000 cubic inches.

Selecting a Vehicle Kit Bag

Your vehicle kit can be a backpack too, but since it doesn't have to be carried for long distances, it could just be a nylon or canvas duffle bag, which is more economical than purchasing an additional backpack. Also, you can often cram more into a duffle bag and even have two or more duffle bags, to carry extra supplies in your vehicle.

An old suitcase or large sports bag can also work well as a vehicle kit bag.

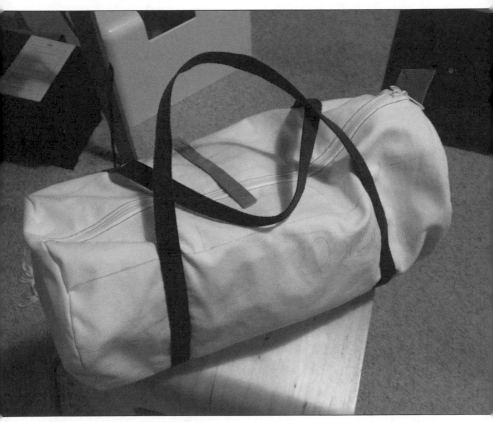

A nylon or canvas duffle makes a great vehicle kit bag. Credit: CC BY 2.0 courtesy of switthoft.

Stocking Your Bug-Out Bag

Water

The first essential is water. You can never have enough water. And depending on the nature of the emergency, you can't always depend on finding water along the way.

Consider that you may need about a gallon a day of water per person. Therefore, fill as many containers with water as you can comfortably carry, with multiple containers (as opposed to large jugs) that will allow you to distribute the weight in your and your family's backpacks.

You also may want to purchase a water bottle that has a

A water bottle that also purifies water can be extremely useful. Credit: CC BY 2.0 courtesy of Tony Webster.

built-in water purifier and water-purifying tablets that you can throw into suspect water. Use the bottled water until you run out. Then, you can use the water-purifying water bottle and tablets for extreme emergency situations.

Food

Food is another essential. Before packing your backpacks, plan your meals. For each person, plan for breakfast, lunch, dinner, and snacks for each day you anticipate traveling to your bug-out destination.

Since you don't know what conditions you'll be facing, you may or may not be able to start a fire to cook food along the way, so food that requires little or no preparation is ideal. You can find camping and "ready-to-eat" meals at your local outdoor and sporting goods store and some government surplus stores. Some of these meals are in "self-heating" packages, so you can have a warm meal even if you can't cook.

However, ready-to-eat meals take up quite a bit of space in your backpack. Depending on the length of your journey, you may want to pack a selection of both ready-to-eat meals and meals that require some cooking. For cooking meals, dehydrated food and food that bulks up when cooked, like rice and oatmeal, are good choices. They take up very little space but produce a filling, satisfying meal.

Also, pack your bag with energy bars and granola bars as well as high-energy foods such as nuts, dried fruits, and jerky. These items have a long shelf life.

First Aid Kit

Every bug-out bag needs a first aid kit. Stock your bag with self-adhesive bandages in a variety of sizes, antiseptic, cotton balls, slings, liquid stitches, and pain reliever pills. You never know what kind of triage you will need to perform, so it also is good to have a booklet on triage and basic first aid so that you can perform CPR, prepare a wound for bandaging, and clean up cuts so that infection does not spread.

Also, remember to pack any prescription medication you are currently taking.

Camping Supplies

If you have a multiday journey ahead of you, it is good to have a few camping essentials in your bug-out bag. Pack a compact backpacking tent, which is a very lightweight tent that is easily carried. If you are bugging out as a family, you may want to carry multiple lightweight tents, rather than one large tent for everyone, as well as a sleeping bag in each person's bug-out kit.

For food preparation, carry a mess kit or hiking cookware, and each person should also have their own utensil kit (knife, fork, and spoon). You may also want a collapsible camping cup for each person.

In addition, you'll want to include a flashlight or backpacking lantern with spare batteries for each person. You may also want matches in a sealed watertight container, a sharp hunting knife, a backpacking saw, a compass, and a pair of work gloves to help with campsite chores. Garbage bags come in handy not just for trash, but any time you need to bag things to keep them separated in your pack, or to keep things from leaking in your pack. A sewing kit may also come in handy along the way.

Other things you might consider packing will depend on where you live and the weather. If it's warm or hot, consider packing sunscreen and/or bug spray. You might also need rain gear such as a compact rain poncho and rain pants.

Carry multiple lightweight tents, rather than one large tent for everyone.

Hygiene Essentials

Pack at least one towel for each member of your family, as well as soap, washcloth, hand sanitizer, and dry shampoo. This way, you'll be prepared if you can bathe with water collected from a river or stream.

If space is at a premium or you don't have access to water along the way to your bug-out location, you can ditch the soap and washcloth. Instead, pack biodegradable camping wipes as a substitute for bathing.

Another idea is packing an empty spray bottle. If you have extra water, you can fill the spray bottle with water to spritz yourself with water to bathe.

You will also need toilet paper and disposable wipes. You can buy hiking toilet paper that does not have a cardboard core and is biodegradable.

And don't forget a toothbrush for each person, as well as toothpaste.

Personal and Protection Items

When bugging out, you'll want to make sure you have copies of all of your important legal documents. These items should not be stored in your bug-out bag, but in a plastic, waterproof container, and placed in your home safe. Then just before leaving, grab the plastic bag from the safe and put it into your bug-out bag.

In this document bag, include either photocopies or scans of your birth certificate, marriage license, wills, real estate and property deeds, auto titles, passports, driver's licenses, social security cards, and any state or federal identification. Also include all insurance papers—home, auto, medical, and life.

Make sure you also have copies of any financial documents and information, such as bank account numbers, credit cards and credit card numbers, debit cards and debit card numbers, and mortgage papers. Remember to bring keys to both your home and any buildings at your bug-out location.

In addition, you'll want to have cash in a variety of denominations, both paper currency and coins. Ideally, you'll want to include lightweight items you can use for barter as well, such as gold and silver coins (both bullion and numismatic collectibles) and jewelry. Again, prepare these items ahead of time and store them in your safe, with your legal papers. Grab them as you are about to bug out.

Speaking of bartering, any extra supplies you can carry,

especially food and water, can also be used to barter along the way if the need arises.

Depending on the magnitude of the emergency, you may also need some protective weapons. At a bare minimum, include pepper spray with your bug-out bag. But as you leave, take it out of the bag and put it someplace you can get to quickly, such as in an easy-to-reach pocket or on a belt loop. (Note: pepper spray is illegal in some areas. Please check your local laws.)

For more serious emergencies, especially if they involve civil unrest, a better item for protection is a handgun, such as a revolver or semiauto pistol. You might also carry a rifle or shotgun, but they are harder to carry and get to than a smaller weapon. So if you carry a long gun, also include a handgun for easy access.

Make sure to bring plenty of spare ammunition. Extra ammunition in common calibers like 9mm (nine millimeters) and .22LR (twenty-two long rifle) may also be useful barter. And make sure everyone in the family is trained in the use and maintenance of all weapons you are bringing.

We'll cover more about firearms and firearm alternatives later in the book, in our section on home security.

But for now, let's talk about packing your bug-out bag.

Packing Your Bug-Out Bag

Keeping things as organized as possible is a rule of thumb for packing your bug-out bag. Although people use different techniques, the main goal in packing items is to keep things in their proper order.

There are backpacks complete with tiny compartments so people can separate light items from heavy ones. When

Pack your bug-out bag so that you can comfortably wear it.

packing, it is good to categorize items that are important for the trip. It is going to be a hassle looking for the things needed when everything is cluttered inside the backpack.

It's important to be sure that things like a compass, rainwear, extra clothing, first aid kit, map, toilet paper, sunglasses, flashlight, food, and drink are easy to access. Put some of these items in the backpack's outside pocket, especially when space is limited.

Stocking Your Vehicle Kit

As I mentioned earlier, I like to use my vehicle kit to supplement my bug-out bag. So while my bug-out bag has the bare essentials, my vehicle kit has additional supplies for a car journey.

First of all, more water and food. The more water you can carry in your vehicle, the better. For food, you can stick with ready-to-eat meals and dehydrated food, but you can also add canned foods, such as meats, soups, chili, beans, and stews. You can also add canned fruits and vegetables, and aseptic-packaged soup, fruit juices, and drinks.

For food preparation, remember to include a can opener for your canned foods. You might want to include a small camping stove, a lighter, and a box of matches in a plastic, resealable bag. Never store lighter fluid or charcoal in a bug-out bag or vehicle kit. These items are highly flammable and can accidently ignite. You can also add plastic utensils, bowls, and cups.

You may also want to include a heavy-duty camping tent and heavier sleeping bags than the ones in your bug-out bag. You may even want a basic tarp and strong rope and stakes for the ground in case you have to rig a shelter on branches in the forest.

In addition, there is one item that you should store separately from your vehicle kit but put in your vehicle just before you leave: extra fuel for the vehicle. Store it in an approved, airtight, leak-proof container for gasoline. Just before you bug out, put it in the trunk of your car (not the passenger compartment) and situate it so that it doesn't spill.

Choosing a Bug-Out Location

ONCE YOU'VE DECIDED TO BUG OUT, YOU NEED TO HAVE AN IDEA of where you are bugging out TO.

In the event of an emergency, a bug-out location (BOL) can help you avoid hardship and, in extreme cases, survive for long periods of time. At a minimum, a good BOL should shelter, feed, and protect your family for up to a month. Ideally, if you can grow food and hunt in the area around your BOL, you could survive there for more extended periods of time.

Buying Property as a BOL

Many people consider a second home or vacation cottage as a perfect choice for a bug-out location. A family member or relative could use the second home as a primary residence during normal times. Some people own vacation cabins, another good option for a retreat during a crisis.

However, you may not be able to afford a second home or a vacation cottage. Another drawback is that in the case of a regional or a national emergency, the situation may also compromise relying on a fixed location for bugging out.

Using an RV as a BOL

Some people own recreational vehicles (RVs) for use during family vacations and other types of travel, especially over long distances. In terms of cost, RVs are less expensive than fixed property like a second home.

One significant advantage of an RV is that it allows you to move to different locations as the situation warrants. RVs vary widely in size and capabilities, with the biggest capable of accommodating a large family.

An RV makes a good bug-out destination but may not be a good bug-out vehicle.

Of course, one consideration in choosing an RV is fuel economy. In an emergency, fuel supplies may not be readily available. One option is to select a hybrid or biodiesel RV, as these options provide more fuel flexibility. You can also use power generation devices like solar panels to charge a hybrid RV's electric motor battery. A biodiesel engine with proper modifications can even run on used cooking oil.

RVs can be vehicles themselves, or they can be trailers that require another towing vehicle. Generally, the trailer variety is cheaper, and you may be able to use your current vehicle for towing.

While an RV might be a good mobile "bug-out" location, it does have some serious drawbacks as a bug-out vehicle. We'll talk more about using an RV when we discuss bug-out vehicles in a later chapter.

Using a Yacht or Houseboat as a BOL

An option similar to that of using an RV, a sizeable live-aboard boat provides mobility, allowing you to move from one docking facility to another, or simply to anchor at practically any location.

Again, fuel is a consideration, and it would be a good idea to ensure that you choose a fuel-efficient craft. Another possibility is to learn how to sail and to purchase a sailboat or a hybrid sail- and motorboat.

Many large boats are capable of long sea voyages and have all the systems, equipment, and storage space needed to keep the occupants sustained for weeks at a time.

Using a Campsite

An even lower-cost option than an RV or boat is to choose one or more campsites as BOLs. All you will need are tents and other equipment included in your vehicle or walking bug-out bag. In some cases, it may even be possible to live out of your car for short periods at these sites.

Like the RV option, camping has the advantage of mobility. In times of crisis, it may be necessary to relocate often to stay safe. Campsites can be good locations for whole support networks to "take over" so that they can maintain mutual security.

One of the disadvantages of camping is that it is not very comfortable over long periods. While you have great mobility, tents do not provide much in terms of fortified protection.

Staying with Friends or Relatives

Of course, this is probably the ideal solution if feasible. However, it is probably more practical for individuals or couples. Not many people have room enough in their home to accommodate an extra family with children.

Another problem is that this option also involves fixed locations, so it is less flexible. One strategy is to set up a network with others in which each member offers their homes to others in case of an emergency. Note that you will need to plan sleeping locations and supply stockpiles.

Camping in the Woods

Camping at national parks, state parks, or on other types of public land is an extreme, but viable, option. In some cases, it may also be possible to camp out on private property with or without the permission of the owner.

Survival in the wilderness requires knowledge of animal and plant life along with other survival skills. An advantage of camping in the woods is that you are less likely to encounter strangers than in more populated areas.

In the woods, it is easy to choose locations where the chances of others randomly finding you are next to nil. However, you must make sure that you have access to water and purification equipment.

Unless you have your own power generation equipment, you will not have electricity, so think about appliances that use solar energy. Solar panels are an option as generators. Biofuel generators are another possibility, and kits are available that allow you to create your own biodiesel or ethanol using plant matter.

An advantage of camping in the wilderness is that you can hunt and fish for food along with gathering wild vegetables, grains, roots, beans, seeds, fruits, and herbs. You could also build a structure using native wood and earth to provide more fortification than is available living in a tent.

Bugging Out on Foot or by Bike

REGARDLESS OF THE REASON FOR EVACUATING, YOU NEED TO BE ready to bug out fast, and with the key items for survival. You can count on most people heading to their cars when it's time to hit the road. That might result in delays as all roadways leaving your area become impossibly congested.

When this happens, you may be able to make better time on foot or by bike. However, bugging out without a motorized vehicle requires special preparations, so you should get everything together ahead of time.

The Benefits of Using Your Feet

You may think that there's no way you would want to evacuate on foot, but there are advantages to this method.

If you're on foot, you'll be limited in the gear you can take, but you won't have to deal with traffic jams. Mechanical breakdowns won't be a concern, and you can go where motorized vehicles cannot. In the event of a full evacuation across a large area, you might get to your bug-out location faster on foot.

Know the Route ahead of Time

In an evacuation, you want to know which route to take ahead of time. Just as you are familiar with the available roadways, you should know the area around your home.

Drainage culverts and small streams are excellent areas to search out and use for bugging out, as they follow reasonably straight lines and will help guide you to another location.

If you live in mountainous regions, the best option may be to head for higher ground and move along the first ridge to the next area. Look for routes that will take you to safer areas faster than congested roads and look for routes with smooth terrain if you will be traveling with children.

Make it a weekend activity to go out and hike these routes with the family for fun, and if you ever need to evacuate, everyone will be more familiar with the terrain, making an evacuation less stressful.

Have Alternate Routes Planned

You may decide that the best route is the one following a stream you've found, but what happens if that area is flooded? Anything can happen, and being prepared means thinking of alternatives ahead of time. Consider the other routes and take the time to hike them. This way, you'll know exactly what to do if your preferred route is blocked due to weather or other hazards.

Take Notes on Your Weekend Hikes

When you are out hiking your escape routes, bring a notebook and a pencil or pen to make notes along the way. Are there natural barriers that will pose problems in an evacuation? Take note of good areas to stop and rest at or even spend the night. How much will weather slow you down given the terrain? Look for areas that are safer and easier to navigate, as well as areas that are more hazardous for some reason.

Determine if there are potential water sources and how well the water could be filtered. Assembling this information ahead of time will allow you to make a faster evacuation when every second counts.

Bike Considerations

Bikes will allow you to travel farther in one day than you could on foot, and you can still go places where cars cannot. If you choose to bug out by bike, then you should invest in some special equipment.

Consider purchasing a bike trailer to carry the gear you need. When traveling with young children, a bike trailer can make the difference between life and death if you have to get out fast and the roads are blocked. Look for trailers designed for the rugged demands of off-road riding.

Make sure you can comfortably wear your bug-out backpack while you are riding, so don't get a backpack that is too big. Go for a smaller backpack and use your trailer or bike bags/saddlebags to carry additional equipment.

Once you have invested in the best bike bags and trailer for your purposes, make sure you pick up a quality light. It will allow you to travel at night, and it makes it easier for your party to stay together. Keep yourself visible to others on the road by installing a small red light in the rear of the bike, ideally one that is easily switched off in case you need to evacuate without drawing attention to yourself.

Bikes aren't useful when tires go flat, and there's a good chance this will happen when you are riding on rough terrain, so take a bike tire repair kit with you and be sure to pack an air

Bugging out on a bike allows you to carry more and travel farther.

pump. Keep a few spare inner tubes on hand, so you won't have to worry about being forced to abandon your bike.

The Single Most Important Item for Bugging Out on Foot

Good shoes. All your preparation for bugging out on foot won't be worth anything if you don't have good shoes for the walk.

A sturdy pair of walking shoes will suffice if your bug-out route is over easy terrain, but if you have a more difficult route, invest in a good pair of hiking shoes or boots. Make sure each member of your family has shoes that fit. If you have kids, you know how quickly they grow, so make sure they have hiking shoes that are the right size.

Take special care of your feet. During rest periods, remove your shoes and socks to let your feet air out and to allow the shoes and socks to dry.

Note: If you are bugging out as a family and in a dangerous situation, you may want to have one or two family members stand guard while the others remove their shoes and socks. After an adequate rest period, switch duties. Taking turns like this will double the amount of time you need for rest periods but may be safer.

During the rest period, remove any dirt, sand, or debris from your shoes. Hang your socks from nearby tree branches to dry and inspect your feet for blisters or signs of rubbing that may turn into blisters. Also, examine one another's feet, because sometimes another person can spot problems before you can.

At the end of the rest period, apply foot cream and adhesive bandages to protect any areas that show signs of rubbing. Change to new socks if you can, rotating through your socks during the trip.

Choosing a Bug-Out Motor Vehicle

Evacuation can be easy with the right bug-out vehicle, so it's crucial to put together a plan for your next vehicle purchase.

Affordability

First and foremost, you'll need an affordable vehicle. If you're like any of the other millions of families, you probably don't have money to throw around wildly.

Keeping in mind vehicle quality, you'll want to look at late-model, used vehicles, as opposed to new vehicles. The money you save by purchasing a used vehicle can be put to better use in other areas of your bug-out plan.

If you find a used vehicle with fewer than 40,000 miles and about three or four years old, it's still like new and would be worth the purchase.

It's standard to have about 10,000 miles a year, so anything higher or lower than that is a bit suspicious and should be treated with caution.

Dependability

Pick a vehicle known for reliability and ruggedness when choosing a bug-out vehicle. It should be easy to repair. Ideally, you should be able to handle some of the repairs yourself, so a vehicle with a simple engine works best. Purchasing a popular model guarantees that more mechanics will know how to fix it, and it will be easier to find spare parts for replacement.

Pick a vehicle that you can drive on a good road, which would make it a viable candidate for doubling as an everyday vehicle. This makes it all the more important to have good gas mileage, so the vehicle will be affordable for daily use as well as for fuel efficient travel away from the disaster.

If you can drive a manual transmission, it's a better choice than an automatic transmission, since manual transmissions are often simpler for a mechanic to fix and use less fuel. You also have more overall control for off-roading.

Off-Road

Though you want to make sure the vehicle handles well on the road, you will also want one that works well off-road. You may need to be able to drive through snow, sand, and mud, even if it accounts for only a small amount of your bug-out driving. There may also be traffic or stranded vehicles in the way, so a four-wheel-drive vehicle is a good choice. Even if you aren't likely to use the off-road capabilities, it's better to have it and not need it than to need it and not have it.

Maneuverability

Finally, select a vehicle that is small rather than large, as these are easier to maneuver around road obstacles like car wrecks or debris. The car needs some power but has to be agile enough for both everyday driving and moving fast in an emergency. Naturally, you'll need something large enough to fit the entire family, but don't overdo it.

Much like getting off-road capability, you'll have to make sacrifices here. For instance, if you have a family, you will need a medium-sized vehicle that can fit five people but isn't too large. You may be able to go for a smaller SUV if you're alone, realizing that you may need the extra room later on.

Considering an RV

When considering bugging out with your family and all of your emergency supplies, you might think of piling everything into your RV, if you have one. However, this may not be the best option when weighing the sacrifices against the potential benefits.

On the positive side, RVs provide great means for stockpiling food and water and can even house you if you don't actually have another emergency shelter. But RVs are large vehicles that don't maneuver very well, even under the best weather conditions.

In addition, they also get abysmal gas mileage, causing frequent stops. In a worst-case scenario, you might not even make it out of town before you need to fill up the tank again. And depending on the emergency, you might find most gas stations closed.

As many potential benefits as there may be, consider the number of bad situations that RVs can cause on the road. For one, you're stuck driving on the main roads, so if your plan to bug out involves driving off-road or you come across a rather large obstacle in the middle of the road, you're going to have trouble in an RV.

There are smaller RVs available, and these may be fine traveling down dirt roads, but true off-road driving would cause too many problems. Smaller RVs are also only a good option if you're by yourself or are very close with a significant other. Once you add children to a smaller RV, there's no more elbow room for any comfort.

Bugging Out with Children and Pets

BUGGING OUT TAKES PLANNING, EVEN WHEN YOU DON'T HAVE kids and pets to consider. However, when you do, it's especially important to make sure that the entire family knows and understands the bug-out plan. We already covered some general advice for prepping with children (see page 61) and pets (see page 66), but read on for tips on bugging out with kids and pets.

For Children

As we said earlier, each member of your family will need a bug-out bag, and that includes your children. Even if they can't carry everything they need, this bag should contain some of their essential items.

And don't underestimate the emotional value of helping your children prepare their bags. Involve them with your preparation plans, and it can help them understand and be less afraid of what might happen during your bug-out. It's also a great way of bonding with your kids and helps them build trust in you. That trust will be important, should you need to lead them on a bug-out.

Of course, only add as much weight to their bug-out bag as

they can carry. But no matter who carries these items, remember to include the following for your infant or children: diapers, wipes, pacifier, crackers, change of clothes, and a comfort blanket or toy.

For Pets

Bugging out with pets is a difficult decision. A lot depends on the way you are bugging out (by foot or by vehicle), and on whether the pet can walk on its own or has to be carried.

I know this is a heartbreaking decision, but if you have to bug out on foot, and the pet has to be carried, it would probably be safer for you to leave the pet behind. The additional weight of carrying the animal may make the entire process more tiring and slow you down. However, please make every effort to either bring your animal or drop them at a shelter, where they have a better chance of survival if you cannot care for them yourself.

But if you do decide to take a pet with you on foot, you'll need to think about how you'll transport your pet. Dogs trained to a leash can walk beside you with a bag or pack on their backs carrying supplies. If it's cold, your dog will need a coat and possibly shoes to protect its feet from rocks, thorns, and similar hazards. Some cats may be able to follow you on a leash, but others you may have to carry in their own carriers, which can be soft-sided for easier transport.

Of course, you'll also need to carry food and water for your pet in your bug-out bag or in his saddlebags. Dry food and treats are easier to carry than canned items. As a general rule, you should plan to bring a half gallon of bottled water for each of your pets each day, although this can vary due to their breed, weight, and other factors. Collapsible bowls will make the load easier to carry.

Bugging out by vehicle offers more possibilities.

During a bug-out situation, your pet will likely feel the stress that you are feeling and react accordingly. When you decide to bug out, you won't have time to round up your pet from his favorite hiding place. That's why it's a good idea to teach him how to get into his carrier or crate on your command. You can then quickly gather essential equipment for both of you instead of wasting precious time trying to coax him into his carrier.

Well before evacuation becomes even a remote possibility, you'll want to spend time training your pet to leave with you calmly.

To help a cat learn to enter a carrier quickly, start putting his favorite blanket or pillow inside on a regular basis so he'll want to sleep there. If the carrier door is held open with a bungee cord, he'll be more likely to enter the carrier freely. Once he's become comfortable doing this, you can start acclimating him to staying in the carrier when you close the door.

Train your pet to get into his carrier or crate on your command for bugging out.

Your dog should learn to come as soon as you call him and allow you to quickly dress him in a coat or sweater and shoes, if necessary. He should be comfortable wearing a harness and backpack over his shoulders and back. He will need time to get used to this before evacuation becomes necessary.

Praise your pet and offer treats when he does these actions with little or no hesitation.

Since you likely won't know where your final destination is or when you'll reach it, you must have enough food and water on hand for your pet in your vehicle kit. As we mentioned, dry food and treats are easiest to carry, but if you must bring canned food, remember to include a manual can opener.

Your pet's veterinary and shot records should travel with you, too. Your pet won't feel comfortable in the area in which you'll likely land, so he may act out and bite or scratch a stranger. In that case, an up-to-date record of his shots is essential to keep him out of trouble. You'll also want to include a copy of his records, especially if he is being treated for an illness or special condition. Finally, a photo of your pet can help identify him if he somehow escapes from you.

Since you're leaving home in an emergency situation, your pet might be injured during the evacuation process. A pet-specific first aid kit will help keep him in good shape until you can see a vet. It should include bandages and gauze, antibiotic ointment, scissors, tweezers, eye wash, ear ointment, and any medications your pet is taking. Flea and tick treatments can also be included, since you may have to travel through wooded areas.

Your pet will need to feel as though something of his familiar home were still available to him during this stressful time. A favorite toy or two and his preferred blanket are great items to quickly place in his carrier as you leave the house. The comforting odors of home will help him relax. Working with your pet well ahead of any emergency situation and providing for his needs and his comfort will help make an unfortunate situation easier for both of you.

Making Sure Your Bug-Out Plan Works

THE BEST WAY TO KNOW IF YOUR BUG-OUT PLAN WORKS IS TO DO trial runs.

Get your family together and go through a pretend bug-out. Pack the vehicle, or grab your bug-out bag and start walking.

Practice makes perfect. For example, with a trial run, you might find there are additional items you need in your bug-out bag that we haven't suggested here. You may find you need items unique to your situation.

Or you might find that the first time you practice, not everything fits in your car! You may have to get better at packing and choosing which items are essential to make the bug-out plan work more easily.

As I said in the previous section on hunkering down, these trial runs will be the best investment you can make in your family's safety. And that's something you just can't put a price tag on.

PART 3

Sealing Yourself In: Prepping for Bioterrorism, Chemical Disasters, and Pandemics

The Scariest Scenarios

"SURVIVAL PREPPERS" WANT TO BE PREPARED FOR ANY emergency.

Whether it's a natural disaster like a hurricane or tornado, or a man-made disaster such as civil unrest or government collapse, we want to be ready. We want to make sure that our families are safe, no matter what catastrophe happens.

In the previous parts of this book, we focused on creating plans for "hunkering down" (living in your home during a disaster) and on "bugging out" (being prepared to evacuate during an emergency). To be fully prepped for anything that happens, you need plans in place both to survive in your home and to leave your home and head to safety.

But of all the things we prep for, there's nothing scarier than biological/chemical disasters. Whether it's an act of deliberate bioterrorism, a rampant pandemic, or an accidental biohazard release, we want to be able to survive no matter what happens.

In this section, we turn our attention to helping you hunker down and survive these more serious disasters.

Speaking of hunkering down, lots of preppers focus on what supplies they need to stockpile for these serious emergencies. But there's one thing that's more important than supplies and plans.

And that is to develop the right mind-set for survival.

What makes us good survival preppers is how mentally prepared we are to face the challenges that may or may not be headed our way in today's world. It's the mind-set that allows us to stop burying our heads in the sand, and to develop the mental focus that puts our family's safety first.

In this part of the book, we're going to focus on information to help you develop the mind-set to face the most frightening survival scenarios out there.

We'll start by looking at the various types of chemical and biological hazards, and the most common bioterrorism agents. And we'll be paying close attention to one of the most common forms of medical emergency throughout history: pandemics.

All of this can be scary reading. It can cause most nonpreppers and even some of us preppers to feel overwhelmed. Especially if you talk to nonpreppers about these subjects, you might find that they go into mental and emotional "shutdown"—as if it were too much information for them to handle. They want to bury their heads in the sand until the overwhelmed feeling goes away.

But for preppers like us, this information is what we want. We want to know what's out there. Yes, there is some scary stuff out there. But learning about it doesn't frighten us. It empowers us, because the more we know, the better our chance of survival.

So if you start reading about all of these hazards and your old "nonprepper" habits of thought creep in, causing you to feel a little overwhelmed, take a moment. Put down the book, take a deep breath, consciously relax your body, and remind yourself why you are here.

You are here because you and your loved ones are depending on you.

Instead of scaring you, let the information on these hazards motivate you. Let it embolden you. Let it strengthen your resolve to be prepared to protect yourself and your family. Let it remind you—that's why you're here. You are a prepper.

After talking about the various types of biological, chemical, and medical dangers, we'll dive in to some details to help you be prepared. We'll look at the items to add to your hunker-down emergency supplies to help you cope as best as you can with bioterrorism, pandemics, and biochemical hazards.

As I wrote earlier, I sincerely hope you NEVER have to use anything I've written here. I pray that you and your family never have to try to survive an act of bioterrorism or a pandemic. But in case you ever do face such a situation, I want to help you be prepared to take care of yourself and your family.

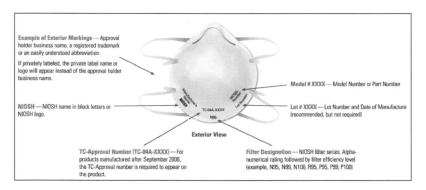

Labels on an N95 mask (see page 136). For more info, go to knowits.NIOSH.gov.

Chemical and Biohazard Emergencies

THE THOUGHT OF TERRORIST ATTACKS AND NUCLEAR THREATS CAN strike fear into your heart and leave you worried for the future. However, there are far more insidious threats out there. The chances are good that you will never have to worry about nuclear fallout, but biological, chemical, and pandemic disasters are very real threats to your safety.

Chemical Dangers

Hazardous chemicals are in use all around us. The military uses nerve agents like sarin and VX ("Venomous agent X"). Industrial manufacturers commonly use chlorine, benzene, and ammonia. Still others, such as those in poisonous plants, are commonly found in nature. Whether the source is intentional in the form of a terror attack, accidental through our manufacturing plants, or from some other cause, the chemicals around us pose real dangers.

From chemicals that blister eyes and burn the respiratory tract to caustic agents that can burn the skin on contact, serious and even fatal health problems can occur. Nerve agents and long-acting anticoagulants that prevent blood from clotting can be fatal.

One of the fears with chemical warfare is that our food supply may be contaminated. While releasing the chemicals in a busy city would certainly be dangerous, the same results can be achieved by destroying the agricultural network and essentially starving the population. Several international treaties have addressed the potential use of these weapons and banned them, but there are still nations working on developing this type of warfare.

Biological, chemical, and pandemic disasters are very real threats to your safety.

In recent decades, terrorists put chemical warfare to use for the first time in history. One memorable event was the release of sarin in Matsumoto, Japan. A year later, sarin vapor was used on the Tokyo subway system during morning rush hour. The attack killed 12 people and caused more than 5,000 injuries. These were small-scale attacks, but they make it clear that larger-scale attacks are possible.

Biohazards

Viruses, medical waste, and toxins are all biohazards that can pose threats to your health. The Center for Disease Control (CDC) breaks biohazards into four different levels, with level 1 being the lowest and level 4 being the most dangerous.

Level 3 biohazards pose a significant risk. They can be fatal if they are not diagnosed and treated in time. Anthrax, West Nile virus, typhus, and malaria are all examples of level 3 biohazards. The most dangerous ones, level 4 biohazards, are generally fatal and are spread easily through both direct contact and the air. Dengue fever and Ebola are examples of level 4 biohazards that threaten your safety.

Even diseases once thought extinct can be used as part of biological warfare. The bubonic plague, which attacks the lymph nodes, is still alive and well, and it is spread through fleas. Other dangerous versions of the plague are the pneumonic plague, which attacks the lungs, and the septicemic plague, which spreads in the blood.

Pandemic Disasters

Largely unavoidable and potentially fatal to large populations, pandemic disasters are nothing new to our modern era. One of the most well-known examples occurred when early settlers in America brought diseases like smallpox, measles, and mumps, to which Native Americans had very little resistance. More recent examples include the Spanish flu of 1918 and the more recent concern about the H1N1 influenza virus.

A pandemic is the massive spread of a disease, whether that disease is known or completely new. While an epidemic simply refers to a disease breaking out, a pandemic refers to a disease that has spread over a larger population.

To see how pandemics spread, let's look at H1N1 as an example. The first case of H1N1 influenza was documented in Mexico in February 2009. Just two months later, in April, the infection was documented in the United States. By May, the virus had spread to other countries, thanks to air travel. By July, there were a million people infected and 429 confirmed deaths from H1N1. A year later, in June 2010, the disease was named as the cause of more than 18,000 deaths worldwide.

As another example, the Spanish flu outbreak of 1918 to 1919 was shorter-lived, but the consequences were more devastating. This disease infected nearly 500 million people, or one-third of the world's population at that time. There were nearly 50 million deaths from this fatal influenza.

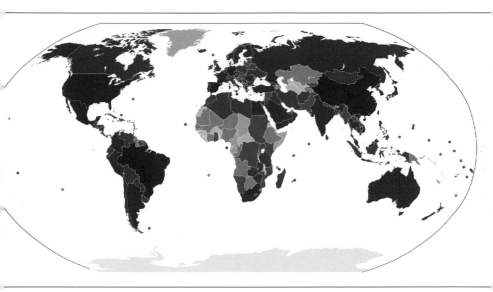

A map showing the reach of the H1N1 influenza virus. Countries shaded with the darkest color, including the United States, experienced upwards of fifty thousand confirmed cases. Credit: HotWikiBR.

Bioterrorism: Agents Used in Intentional Attacks

BIOTERRORISM IS A SPECIAL CONCERN IN THIS DAY AND AGE. AND there is a seemingly endless supply of possible bioterrorism agents. Many of these agents come from natural sources. Some agents are aerosolized for dissemination in public places.

Knowing more about symptoms and different types of bioterrorism agents can prepare you in the event of a possible attack.

Bioterrorism Agent Categories

The Center for Disease Control (CDC) has three separate categories for bioterrorism agents. The agents can be classified depending upon how easily they spread and how severe they are. Category A is for bioterrorism agents that pose the greatest risk to public health. Category B is the next most dangerous, with Category C following behind.

The following list includes some of the more dangerous types of bioterrorism agents listed in Category A:

Anthrax

Anthrax is caused by contact with spores of the *Bacillus Anthracis* bacterium. These spores can infect people through skin, lungs, or digestive tract. You can contract anthrax from animals, especially from the wool of infected sheep. Another way to get anthrax is from eating undercooked meat of animals that may have been infected.

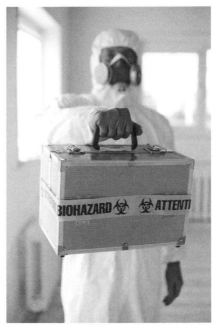

Bioterrorism agents pose a great risk to public health.

Weaponized anthrax is typically done by milling it into a fine powder. The 2001 anthrax attacks were weaponized this way and sent through the mail. The CDC puts anthrax in category A. This makes anthrax one of the more dangerous bioterrorism agents. The deadliest form of anthrax is contracted through the lungs. Symptoms generally occur within a week.

It is important to recognize anthrax symptoms as soon as possible. The cutaneous (skin) form of anthrax usually develops like a blister with a black center. The gastrointestinal form of anthrax is accompanied by bloody diarrhea, nausea, and bad stomach pains.

If you inhale anthrax, the symptoms may resemble that of a flu or cold at first. Symptoms will increase in severity if not treated immediately. An aggressive antibiotic schedule in conjunction with the anthrax vaccine is the treatment for exposure.

Botulism

Botulism remains one of the deadliest toxins. *Clostridium botulinum* is the bacterium responsible for causing botulism. Botulism is typically ingested from contaminated foods. Botulism paralyzes the muscles in your body. Eventually, you will be unable to swallow, and you will need a mechanical ventilator for breathing.

If you suspect botulism, immediate medical attention is crucial. Symptoms usually occur between 12 and 36 hours after exposure. The CDC does have a stockpile of antitoxin in the event of a public outbreak. Long-term supportive care may be necessary for recovering patients.

Pneumonic Plague

Yersinia pestis is the bacterium that causes a severe lung infection. Within a week of exposure, you may have flu-like symptoms. The symptoms get increasingly severe and generally end with respiratory failure and death. The ability of *Yersinia pestis* to be aerosolized makes it a possibility for bioterrorism attacks.

There are a few naturally occurring cases of the plague each year in the United States. If you think you may have the plague, it is important to seek medical attention immediately. An aggressive antibiotic schedule can be used, if you seek medical attention within the first 24 hours after symptoms appear. Quick intervention can drastically improve your chances of living through this disease.

It is possible to contract this disease from another infected person. The CDC reports that federal and state government health organizations have large amounts of antibiotics ready in the event of a bioterrorist attack.

Smallpox

Smallpox is another possible agent that could be used in the event of a bioterrorism attack. The last case of smallpox in America occurred over 60 years ago. Smallpox is generally considered a disease of the past. The federal government is taking precautions for treatment in the event of a bioterrorism attack.

Smallpox is characterized by the spotted rash that accompanies the disease. *Variola major* is the most common type of the disease, with an average incubation period of about 12 to 14 days. After this incubation period, you will begin to display initial symptoms. The initial symptoms are flu-like. Following a few days of initial symptoms, you will begin to see a rash.

Smallpox hasn't been a worldwide concern since the 1970s. Aggressive vaccination procedures effectively eradicated the disease. The CDC states that there are enough vaccinations stockpiled in the event of a possible bioterrorism attack.

Tularemia

Tularemia has also been called "rabbit fever." This disease is typically seen in rural communities where people may have contact with infected rabbits or rodents. *Francisella tularensis* is the bacterium that causes tularemia. The possibility of infection from an airborne version of this bacterium makes it a possible bioterrorism threat.

Symptoms of tularemia can include skin ulcers, sore throat, diarrhea, painful swollen lymph nodes, and inflamed eyes. Symptoms can get progressively worse, and this disease can turn fatal if not treated. An antibiotic schedule is necessary for successively treating tularemia. Early intervention is important for treatment and recovery.

Viral Hemorrhagic Fevers

Viral hemorrhagic fevers such as Ebola or hantavirus could be incredibly dangerous if used as bioterrorism weapons. The viruses that cause these types of illnesses are often zoonotic—that is, they can jump from animals to humans or from humans to animals.

Symptoms of viral hemorrhagic fevers are often flu-like at first. Symptoms progress and usually also include internal bleeding and bleeding under the skin. Complications in advanced-stage patients include coma, shock, seizures, and nervous system malfunction.

For many viral hemorrhagic fevers, there are no known cures. Supportive therapy is usually the only course of treatment. The most important thing is to avoid coming into contact with an infected host. Rodent and insect control is important in areas where infected host animals reside.

Arming yourself with knowledge is crucial in the event of a bioterrorism attack. Many experts agree that the above listed agents are likely to inflict the most damage in the event of an attack.

More about Pandemics

OF ALL THE POSSIBLE BIOLOGICAL, MEDICAL, AND CHEMICAL scenarios, pandemics are certainly the most common throughout history. We spoke a little about pandemics earlier (see page 116), but let's look at them in more detail now.

Phases

A pandemic disease is one that is highly infectious and can spread through the population across a large area. Affecting more people than epidemics do, pandemics have been characterized as having six phases by the World Health Organization (WHO). Knowing these phases and understanding what they mean can save your life in the event of an outbreak.

Phase 1 indicates the virus is being seen in animals, but it has not yet moved into the human population.

Phase 2 means that the virus has moved into humans and officially become a pandemic threat.

Phase 3 indicates that the disease has been found in small groups of humans, but it has not yet become contagious among people.

Phase 4 is the point at which the disease is being transmitted among people and indicates a heightened risk of pandemic outbreak.

Phase 5 is the point where the spread of the disease among

humans has breached country borders and is in two or more countries.

Phase 6 is the most serious. It indicates that the disease is a pandemic with global reach, affecting three or more countries.

Influenza Pandemics

Influenza or flu viruses have caused some of the most serious pandemics in the past. The flu virus is typically broken up into three different categories—A, B, and C—with influenza A being the most likely to cause extensive and severe outbreaks.

Influenza A viruses will affect both humans and animals, making widespread contagion much more likely. Influenza B

Pandemics now spread very quickly through international travel.

viruses, on the other hand, only affect humans; and for the most part, influenza C simply stops at mild respiratory discomfort.

An influenza A virus is the most likely to cause a pandemic because the methods of transmission may cross the species border and can be spread back and forth among people. Examples of influenza A outbreaks include swine flu and avian flu.

SARS

SARS is the abbreviation for Severe Acute Respiratory Syndrome, and this pandemic occurred between 2002 and 2003. During the course of its run, it was responsible for almost a thousand deaths.

SARS is considered an influenza A virus, with the origins of the virus starting with the spread of the disease from small animals to people. After that, however, the main cause of the disease's spread was through simple human sneezing and coughing.

On top of that, the virus was resilient enough to be passed through touching a contaminated surface and then touching the nose, eyes, or mouth. SARS is treated in a number of ways, including antibiotics, medications, and steroid injections, which can reduce the swelling and the inflammation in the lungs.

HIV and AIDS

Both Human Immunodeficiency Virus (HIV) and Acquired Immunodeficiency Syndrome (AIDS) are pandemics of global proportions.

HIV was originally thought to be a result of contamination from Old World, nonhuman primates. Among humans, the major source of the disease's spread is through sexual contact, though before it was well understood, there were many other vectors for the disease. Organ transplant was once a source for HIV transmission, as were other medical practices.

According to the most recent reporting, as many as 34 million people around the world have HIV, and over the course of the disease's outbreak, almost 30 million people have died from complications with the disease. Though the number of deaths from AIDS has decreased, dropping from 3.1 million deaths in 2001 to 1.8 million deaths in 2010, it is still considered a serious pandemic.

The Black Death (Bubonic Plague)

Though the word *pandemic* seems like a modern idea, the truth is that history is rife with pandemics. Since the 1500s, there have typically been on average three pandemics every century, though they are not at all equal in terms of mortality, spread, and death toll.

One example of a historic pandemic is the famous black death, known in the modern era as the bubonic plague, which had a death toll that is commonly numbered at around 25 million, though some historians consider the death toll to be much higher.

The disease swept through Asia to the Mediterranean, and from there it went north to Western Europe. The disease's spread was facilitated by cross-contamination with fleas and rodents. The plague was said to have lasted for three hundred years, with some of the outbreaks lasting for years at a time in certain places.

Interestingly enough, the bubonic plague is still a disease that breaks out from time to time in the modern era. If it is caught within the first 24 hours, it is entirely treatable by modern antibiotics.

The Real Risk of Pandemics

Whether they are mild or severe, pandemics are not events to be taken lightly. With international travel being so prevalent, viruses can cross boundaries and vast distances more easily than they ever could before. This means that it is possible to spread diseases very quickly, especially when you consider time spent at an airport or any other travel hub.

Pandemics are a serious issue that can take on startlingly real effects in a very short amount of time. If you are someone who is invested in emergency preparedness, it is very important that you understand the risk of pandemics, especially when other disasters may be going on. For example, due to the decreased hygiene and sanitation that usually occurs during a disaster situation, contagion becomes more likely.

Your Armory against Chemical, Biological, and Pandemic Threats to You and Your Family

ALL OF THIS PAST DISCUSSION MIGHT MAKE BIOLOGICAL, CHEMICAL, and pandemic threats seem almost invincible. But there are measures that you and your family can take to prepare for your safety to prevent or at least reduce the impact of these agents.

Ironically, in the war against these highly complicated dangers, the best defensive weapons are actually quite simple to obtain and easy to use.

How to Seal Your Home

It is essential to seal your house during many biological and chemical disasters, as well as some pandemics. This keeps you and your family safe from contaminants.

If you are coming from outside your home, you should remove all exposed clothes and accessories before going indoors. Leave all these things outside. This keeps you from contaminating your home if you have come in contact with the toxin.

Immediately take all family members and pets inside.

Ensure that they also remove their clothing and accessories. Everyone in the household should shower and clean their bodies to remove any toxins.

Things that you need in sealing your home include the following.

- Duct tape
- Scissors
- Plastic sheeting

You will need to cover all doors, windows, vents, and any openings in your house.

To seal yourself in, cover all openings in your home with plastic sheeting and duct tape. This example shows sealing a window from the outside, but in a contagion scenario, you would seal openings from the inside. Credi: US Air Force photo/Staff Sgt. Nathan Bevie.

Before starting, put on an N95 mask. (N95 masks are discussed on page 136.)

Lock all doors and windows, except the front door. Locking will keep the doors and windows sealed tighter to allow fewer contaminants to go into your home. However, leave the front door unlocked in case emergency crews need to enter.

Make sure to close fireplace dampers and places where air from outside can enter. Turn off air-conditioning, fans, heating, and vents.

To secure any opening, first use duct tape to tape over any seams in the opening. For example, on a window, place duct tape over where the window meets the sill and window frame. On a covered vent, tape over any place the cover meets the wall or ceiling. On a door, tape around where the door meets the frame. Make sure to cover all areas around the hinges, as these are usually not airtight.

Once you've taped the seams, cover the opening with plastic sheeting. Inexpensive plastic polyethylene sheeting is often available at "dollar stores" and hardware stores. In a pinch, you can tape together plastic garbage bags, or use plastic shower curtain liners or even painter's plastic drop cloths.

Use scissors and/or tape to create plastic sheets that are the correct size for each opening. Place the plastic sheets over the openings and secure them with duct tape. It's better to use too much tape than too little.

Creating a Quarantine Room

If you or a family member has been exposed during this emergency, it is important to keep them away from those who have not been exposed. Create a quarantine room in order to isolate any exposed family members.

Choose a room in your house, preferably a bedroom, to use as the quarantine room.

Ideally, it should be a room with as few windows and openings as possible. In addition, the quarantine room should have its own bathroom. If it doesn't, place a "honey bucket" or chemical toilet in the room.

Also, put in the room 72 hours' worth of food and water for each person you are quarantining. If you have bug-out bags prepared, you can put the bug-out bag in with the family member. Make sure there are N95 masks for each person in the room. (N95 masks are discussed on page 136.)

To create the quarantine room, place all the supplies in the room first. Then put on your own N95 mask and seal all of the doors, windows, and vents except for the entrance door. Follow the instructions above on how to seal these openings.

Once everything but the entrance door is sealed, have your exposed family members put on their N95 masks and enter the room. Once they are in, exit the room and cover the entrance door from the outside with duct tape and plastic sheeting.

Soap and Water

During many of these disasters, and especially during pandemics, the best way to defend yourself and your family is sometimes with just plain old soap and water. It may be trite, it may be boring, but washing your hands thoroughly and frequently is one of the survival prepper's secret weapons.

In most cases, contagious illnesses must enter the body in order to make a person sick. By simply making a habit of washing your hands and making sure that your family does the same, you are drastically reducing the danger of contracting contagious illnesses, including those of large-scale proportions.

When hand washing is not possible, an alcohol-based hand sanitizer is very effective at killing germs. Hand sanitizer doesn't always remove solid particles, so it should only be used to supplement hand washing, not replace it.

Exposure Procedure

In the rare situation where you are exposed to dangerous chemicals or a biological weapon, soap and water can save your life.

Immediately after exposure, clothing, glasses, contact lenses, and jewelry should be removed. Shirts should be cut off, as opposed to being lifted over your head, in order to reduce the risk of inhaling the offending chemical.

Once your clothing, glasses, contact lenses, and jewelry are removed, they need to be sealed in a plastic bag and thrown away. It may be possible to reuse eyeglasses and jewelry after they are thoroughly rinsed, but it would be better to discard them. For eyeglasses, always have a spare pair or two with your emergency items.

It is crucial that you rinse your body within a few minutes of exposure to the substance, and to do so before you enter your home. Once you are completely stripped (now is NOT the time for modesty), use your outdoor garden hose to thoroughly wash yourself with soap and water for 10 to 15 minutes.

If you believe that there is a possibility that any of the powder, liquid, or vapor may have gotten in your eyes, rinse them with running water for 10 minutes. Use soap and running water to remove any residue from your skin as promptly as possible to reduce the amount that is absorbed.

Once you are clean, put on freshly laundered, noncontaminated clothes. Go immediately into your house, and into your quarantine room if necessary.

Hygiene

Hygiene is a primary consideration when you deal with these types of disasters. In addition to soap and hand sanitizers, make sure you have plenty of toilet paper, facial tissues, deodorant, and disinfectants like chlorine bleach with your emergency supplies.

If water is not available for human waste, use "honey buckets" (a bucket designed for capturing and storing human waste), or place garbage bags over your toilet bowl to catch and dispose of waste. Use baking soda or quicklime to help cut down on odor and neutralize the waste.

And make sure you keep your waste at least one hundred feet away from your food and water.

Air Filters

In the case of an airborne threat, a HEPA filter can reduce the danger within your home or office. Although a HEPA filter cannot stop a chemical weapon from wreaking havoc, it can prevent the spread of disease.

If your home or office has a central heating and cooling system, HEPA filters can be attached directly to the system. If you do not have such a system, a freestanding unit can also be used.

A freestanding HEPA air filter can also be put into your quarantine room. It will maintain the air quality of the room for your exposed family members.

Food and Water

In the direst of circumstances, it is possible that basic services will be reduced or even cease altogether. It is important to have food and water stored for such a situation.

Earlier in this book, we recommend a minimum 10-day supply of food and water. Of course, 30 days would be better, and even up to a year is ideal. But start with a 10-day supply, and you can build up from there.

In part one of this book, we went into great detail about prepping your home emergency supplies. But as a quick refresher, here are the basics.

Store three gallons of water per day, per person (for drinking water, bathing, and washing dishes). This water should be stored in appropriate containers in a dry and cool place. Store it away from chemicals or other possible contaminants. Make sure you change this water out every six to 12 months with fresh water.

Stock your emergency food larder with any foods that have a long shelf life and don't require refrigeration. Canned foods are ideal, such as meats, soups, chili, beans, and stews. Also include canned fruits and vegetables, as well as aseptic-packaged soups, juices, and drinks. Other items you might want to include are dried nuts, peanut butter, energy bars, granola bars, dry cereals, and canned milk. You might also include dehydrated "camping meals" and MRE ("Meals Ready to Eat") packages from your local outdoor or sporting goods store.

All of these items can be eaten without heating. While you may be able to cook during some pandemics, as a precaution, you should never use stoves or anything that uses fire during biological and chemical disasters. Some of these agents may be flammable. In addition, in a sealed home, there is a risk of poor ventilation from items like camp stoves and sterno burners.

Make sure to regularly check expiration dates of your stored foods. You should also replace products that are nearly expired to replenish your supply.

Remember to include a can opener with your emergency supplies, plus eating utensils such as plastic knives, forks and spoons, plates, and paper cups. You'll also want dish soap for cleanup.

First Aid Kit

A first aid kit is necessary in all emergency situations. Family members are prone to injuries and sickness during these disasters. Your kit should include all necessary medicines and equipment. It should have all the things needed for wound care. Also include a booklet on first aid techniques.

Make sure your first aid kit includes:

- Bandages, cotton pads, elastic wraps, gauze, and medical tape. These items will help in the event that any abrasions or sprains occur. A box of "skin closure strips" can help close larger cuts.
- Rubbing alcohol, peroxide, and witch hazel. These can all be used to clean wounds.
- Aspirin. This will reduce fevers and ease pain.
- Antidiarrhea medications. Many biological and pandemic episodes will have diarrhea associated with the effects of the virus. Having this type of over-the-counter medication will be quite useful.
- Multivitamins. You should have multivitamins packed so that all people affected can maintain their strength. You may not be able to eat healthy during this period, and vitamins will ensure you stay well nourished.
- Cough and cold medicines. A multipurpose medicine will come in handy if symptoms arise.
- Soap. Make sure that you have bars of soap in your

medical supplies. It will be very important to clean your hands in the event of bioterrorism or pandemic.

- Prescription medications. If you have time to prepare for the event, call your doctor and request an extra month of your prescription medications.

N95 Masks

An N95 mask (also called an N95 "particulate respirator") is an air-purifying mask. The "95" means that the mask will filter out 95 percent of small, airborne particles. These masks are helpful when airborne biological or chemical contaminants are present.

N95 masks should be tight-fitting to be effective. It may be difficult to get a tight seal on younger children and on adults

N95 masks filter out 95 percent of small, airborne particles.

with facial hair. N95 masks also do not provide complete protection. But if you combine their use with proper hygiene and regular hand washing, you greatly reduce the risk of infection during a pandemic.

Note that an N95 mask is not the same as a surgical mask. A surgical mask only blocks large particles, not small particles. In addition, surgical masks are designed to protect other people from the person wearing the mask. If you put a surgical mask on someone who is sick, it may give some protection to those around the ill person. But putting a surgical mask on someone who is well does not protect them from someone who is sick.

You can find N95 masks online. Keep a good supply on hand for the whole family. These masks are disposable and not for long-term use. A mask should be discarded if it becomes soiled, damaged, or torn, or if it no longer fits tightly.

Communications

For biohazards and pandemics, we don't usually expect electricity or utilities to be disrupted. So you may still have access to your landline phone, television, and even the internet for communication.

However, in case the pandemic does disrupt utilities, you may wish to have, at a minimum, a cell phone and a battery-powered transistor radio to stay in touch with the situation. Don't forget to have external batteries or extra charged batteries for your mobile phone, as well as extra batteries for the radio.

Additional options for communications are ham radios, CB Radios, and walkie-talkies. Check the first part of this book for more details.

General Equipment

You should also include in your emergency supplies:

- Flashlights or lanterns. You should always have battery-powered flashlights or lanterns with extra batteries available. As a precaution, never use candles during biochemical emergencies. Some biological and chemical agents can be highly flammable.
- Baby wipes. These are perfect for keeping things clean when you do not have access to running or clean water.
- Toiletries. You should have a supply of toiletries on hand that will allow you to maintain your cleanliness for at least a month. This includes toilet paper, tissues, feminine products, shampoo, soap, shaving cream, and toothpaste.
- Diapers and baby supplies. You should have a supply of diapers and infant formula on hand at all times.
- Children's supplies, especially favorite pillows, blankets, and clothing.
- Pet supplies. If you are sheltering with your pet, don't forget his or her needs: food and water, medicine, first aid kit, flea and tick treatments, litter, newspapers, trash bags, toys, and treats.
- Tool Box. Simple tools such as a hammer, a few screwdrivers, nails, screws, pliers, and a wrench should be in your kit.
- Buckets, bottles, and containers. You can use these for storing food, water, and waste.
- Board games and entertainment for the family. Children can be restless, and that will be an

inconvenience. Make sure to have board games or other fun activities that can keep your children busy and occupied.

These are the essential items for sealing yourself in during biological and chemical disasters. Once again, for additional ideas on how to prepare for surviving in your home, check the first part of this book.

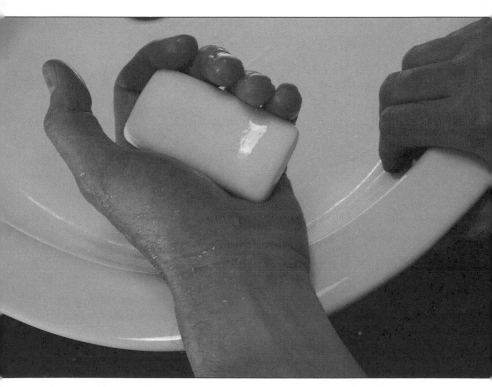

It may be trite, but washing your hands thoroughly and frequently is one of the survival prepper's secret weapons.

Pandemics in Non-quarantine Situations

FOR SOME PANDEMICS, YOU MAY NOT NEED TO SEAL YOURSELF IN your home. As a matter of fact, your normal daily activities may actually continue during pandemics. But you may need to take special precautions during the pandemic to prevent you or your family from becoming infected.

You should first identify the kind of pandemic that is present in your area. You can listen to or watch the news to get information.

There are different kinds of diseases that can cause a pandemic. The three main types are waterborne, airborne, and vectorborne. Each kind of pandemic has its own precautionary measures. You should be able to avoid getting infected by knowing what the pandemic is and learning how to survive it without getting infected.

Waterborne Pandemics

Cholera is an example of a waterborne disease that has caused pandemics. Cholera pandemics are commonly found in third world countries, and there have been numerous accounts of these pandemics all over the world. This disease has also hit areas in Europe and America, causing the deaths of over 300,000 people.

Mode of Transmission

Cholera and other waterborne pandemics spread through water and foods. This disease can be easily transferred when a person with cholera prepares food. If the water supply gets contaminated, all households in the area are in danger of being infected. A number of pandemic cholera outbreaks are spread through water supplies.

Things to Consider

Because waterborne pandemics like cholera can spread through foods and liquids, it is best to be careful with your intake. You should keep enough food to last your family for at least a month. Make sure to regularly check the food supply for expiration dates and consume the ones that are nearly expired first.

Since you won't be sealed in your home, cooking will usually be available, and all food should be thoroughly cooked. If you buy food prepared in restaurants, you should cook it again to destroy any bacteria present.

You should store bottles of clean water if possible. The water supply is not always safe for drinking during an outbreak and may even be unsafe for washing and cooking.

You may be able to purify the water by boiling and chlorination. The basic process is to boil the water for five to 10 minutes, then allow it to cool. Add about one-eighth of a teaspoon of standard, nonscented household chlorine bleach per gallon of water. Shake it thoroughly and then allow it to set for at least 30 minutes. This may work for most waterborne pandemics, but watch the news or listen to the radio for specific details on how to do this for the pandemic specific to your area.

It is also important to wash your hands before preparing

food with safe water. You should also wash your hands when you get home and after going to the bathroom. This will stop the transmission of cholera and keep you and your family safe.

Airborne Pandemics

Influenza pandemics have long been the cause of thousands of deaths worldwide. The Asiatic flu, Spanish flu, Hong Kong flu, and bird flu are some of the recognized influenza pandemics

Pandemics have been with us throughout history and still threaten us today.

that have hit worldwide. This kind of pandemic usually spreads quickly, as the diseases are airborne. You can be infected by an influenza virus even without physical contact.

Other airborne diseases like Severe Acute Respiratory Syndrome (SARS) and tuberculosis have also caused widespread pandemics. These diseases have caused the death of over 100 million people in the 20th century.

Mode of Transmission
Different strains of the influenza virus are spread through the air. Some strains can infect a person as far as a few meters away. On the other hand, some people get infected from nasal and oral secretions. You usually need to be really close to the infected person to get the virus.

Things to Consider
Tuberculosis, influenza, and coronaviruses are airborne and can easily infect you. One precautionary measure is to stay at home and avoid unnecessary bodily contact with other people. You should also avoid populated areas. Thoroughly wash your hands with soap and water after handling objects.

You should always cover your nose and mouth when sneezing or coughing. After sneezing or coughing, dispose of used tissues properly. Make sure not to touch or come in contact with other people's secretions.

If you need to go outside, you should wear approved masks like an N95 mask. This will purify the air you breathe and keep you from being infected. The influenza virus will not be able to pass through the mask's material.

If you are developing flu-like symptoms, you should stay home and not have physical contact with other people. You should monitor your condition and take necessary medications. Antiviral medications that are made to counter influenza viruses are available in pharmacies.

It is also important to stay updated on the pandemic's development. Watch the news or listen to the radio to learn about the specific strain of the virus or bacteria. You should take the appropriate safety measures to protect yourself and your family.

Pandemics Transmitted by Vectors

Vectors are organisms that transmit diseases from one host to another. Common vectors are invertebrates like mosquitoes. They spread diseases through their bites and feces.

Although vector diseases like malaria are commonly found in tropical and subtropical areas, a few temperate areas have also had malaria outbreaks. Historically, malaria caused a pandemic called Roman fever that contributed to the fall of the Roman Empire. This disease also infected people in America during the Civil War. It caused infections in over one million soldiers.

Mode of Transmission

Mosquitoes that get infected and spread the disease are females in the *Aedes Aegipti* genus. They spread pandemics like malaria and dengue fever through their bite. The mosquito will also lay infected eggs. These will hatch and spread the disease.

Things to Consider

The best way to prevent these diseases is to make sure your home is free of disease-bearing insects. Spray your home with bug sprays and insect killers, following the manufacturer's instructions.

Outdoor ponds and water supplies should be covered, as mosquitoes lay their eggs in water. When these eggs hatch, the larvae look similar to frog tadpoles but have a distinctive jerky, "shimmy" style of movement that is different from that of tadpoles. Make sure to drain unnecessary pools of water outside your house.

You should also use insect repellent when outdoors. Have your children use the repellent BEFORE going out of the house. It is also best to wear long pants and long-sleeved shirts to protect yourself from mosquito bites.

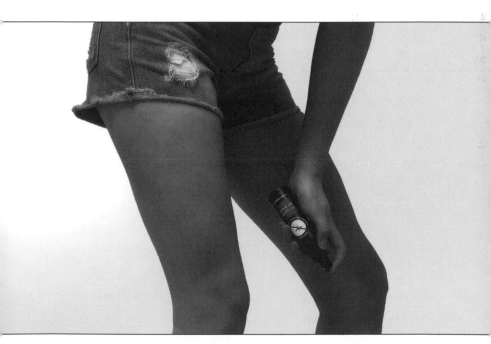

Apply insect repellent before going out of doors during an insect-borne pandemic.

PART 4

Situational Prepping

Situational Awareness in the Modern World

AS EACH DAY PASSES, WE SEE MORE AND MORE INSTANCES OF terrorism, mass shootings, riots, and other "mob" events taking place around the world. Drivers plowing into crowds, terrorists firing into crowds of people, and extreme acts of violence and hatred are becoming more and more commonplace.

Every single thing that you can do to increase your family's chances of survival in an out-of-control world should be considered part of your survival preparation. So now is the time to develop and hone your skills in the area of situational awareness.

What Is Situational Awareness?

What do we mean by situational awareness? Simply put, situational awareness is having a purposeful, alert awareness of your surroundings in order to be prepared to react to any possible dangers.

Daily application of situational awareness will increase your chances of survival and will decrease the likelihood of panic or inappropriate responses when faced with an unexpected life-or-death situation.

Beware of crowds of strangers whose intentions and reactions are unknown.

Situational Awareness in Daily Life

Let's look at an example of how to apply this in daily life. You and your family decide to attend a local gathering, such as a sporting event, a concert, or a fair.

Should you go unprepared into a situation like this, where you know there will be crowds of strangers whose intentions and reactions are unknown?

Obviously not, considering that some of the strangers at this event may have bad intentions. You may have people there who are planning on stealing from others, such as pickpockets planning to steal wallets or cell phones. Some may be there to harm others in order to draw attention to themselves or to their cause. And some may be there intending to hurt or kill others for some twisted psychological motive. And you never know when a gathering of people will turn into an unruly mob in the blink of an eye.

So what sort of preparations can you make in this situation?

Let's start by thinking about traveling to the event. For example, if you are driving, you may know a number of different routes to get to the location. Determine which route works best for you.

You'll want to avoid congestion, as well as avoid those drivers who don't know the area and can cause traffic jams. If something happens before you even arrive at the event, you may need to get away quickly. You don't want other drivers who will impede your escape.

So your situational awareness here might suggest that you choose side roads to reach the event, rather than the main route that most people will use.

Next, when you arrive, you'll have to determine where to park. Is parking close to the event a good choice? Usually not. Yes, it's convenient, but what if something unfortunate happens and you need to leave the event quickly? You could find yourself in a traffic jam unable to move, because everyone else is trying to leave at the same time.

So even if you have to walk a distance, parking away from the event will usually provide a better means of getting away quickly should you need to do so.

Of course, you'll want to be "situationally aware" of your parking location, as well. You'll want to make sure that you are parking someplace safe, so that you decrease the likelihood that your vehicle may be broken into or stolen while you are at the event. You'll also want to park somewhere near good lighting if you are planning to stay after dark at the event, to decrease the likelihood that someone may hide in the shadows and attempt to rob you as you return to your car.

These are just a few examples of the decisions you'll need to make to be aware of the situation—and you haven't even reached the event yet!

This type of thinking—where you consider all of the "what ifs," all of the planning for different variables, and how you would react to each—is part and parcel of situational awareness.

You are creating a mind-set in yourself to make this type of thinking second nature. This makes you much more likely to react appropriately when faced with a dangerous situation. It also makes it much more likely for you to remain calm, cool, and collected just when you most need to be. This kind of cool-headed thinking helps you make the best decisions to keep your family (and, possibly, innocent victims nearby) safe at that moment.

Practicing Your Situational Awareness

Of course, a sporting event, concert, or fair is a special event. Because we often know about these events ahead of time, we can plan ahead. But in our everyday life, we don't always have time to plan this carefully.

Still, we can use everyday situations—ones that occur more spontaneously or randomly during our day—to practice our situational awareness. From these more everyday events, you can develop a number of skills that will keep you safe in a wide variety of circumstances.

Let's look at an everyday example. You stop at a branch of

your bank, in an unfamiliar town, because you need to handle a transaction with a clerk's assistance.

As you enter the bank, take a moment to orient yourself to your surroundings.

Where are the nearest exits, in addition to the one that you just came through? (This creates an awareness of physical environment and enables an evaluation of ways to escape possible imminent threat of harm.)

Scan the people in the vicinity. Make note of who you see and what they are doing. Does anyone seem out of place? Sketchy? Too nervous for the situation? (This hones your innate awareness of potential threats so you can evaluate how to handle same.)

As you await your turn at the counter, take a moment to imagine something bad going down. What if that man standing near the door with a small backpack at his feet suddenly pulls out a gun and fires into the air, yelling for everyone to get down? What would you do? (This serves as mental preparation for worst-case scenarios.)

What if, instead, a vehicle suddenly plows through the plate glass window in the front of the bank? Which way would you go to avoid being struck by the car? Can you help someone nearby reach safety, as well? (This creates a mind-set of looking at all the options available to you in a time of crisis.)

This type of exercise can be applied to a wide variety of everyday situations. Your situational awareness training will prepare your mind and body to react quickly and appropriately when faced with any type of danger.

In the upcoming chapters, we'll discuss how to apply your situational awareness to more difficult situations that can occur in public places. But before we do that, let's discuss the biggest impediment to situational awareness.

Your Biggest Impediment to Situational Awareness

A smartphone is your biggest impediment to situational awareness.

Although smartphones are a very useful part of your disaster preparedness tools, most members of society tend to allow their surroundings to vanish as they become engrossed in their cell phone.

We've all seen videos of people walking into walls, into busy streets, even falling into sidewalk holes, all because they are so involved in looking at the tiny screens of their cellular devices that they have allowed the rest of the world to disappear. They have totally lost all awareness of their surroundings.

As you develop your family's situational awareness skills, be mindful that this is one serious issue you will need to consider, especially if you have children or teens in your household.

If you have to use a cell phone in a public place, stop a moment before you use it. I suggest actually putting it away at this point. Put it in your pocket or purse. Then do your situational awareness. Evaluate the location and the people first. Only after you have a good read on the situation should you then pull out your cell phone to use it.

Even while you are using your cell phone, get in the habit of pausing, looking around, and reassessing the situation every so often.

Depending on the situation, you'll want to redo your situational awareness every two to five minutes. Even in the safest situations, I would go no longer than five minutes without reevaluating the situation.

I like to make sure I drop my hand, taking my cell phone

down away from my face, to remind me to look around. I actually put the cell phone down next to my leg and tap it against my thigh. It helps me condition myself using a physical "signal" that reminds me that I should be reassessing the situation.

Hopefully you have seen the wisdom of making situational awareness part of your normal skills training in order to augment your daily preparation for whatever may come your way. If you incorporate this type of training into your routine, you will increase your mental acuity, enhance your ability to deal with unplanned events, and develop confidence and peace of mind. You'll know that you are doing all that you can to ensure that you act confidently and appropriately should you face danger head-on.

Situational awareness is a skill that you can teach your children, family members, and friends in order to create confidence and ensure that they be mentally prepared in any situation.

Now let's move on to discuss some specific situations where you can use your new situational awareness skills.

Surviving Mass Shootings and Terrorist Attacks

TERRORIST ATTACKS, BOTH IN THE UNITED STATES AND ABROAD, have given us a glimpse of the dangerous world we live in. The twin-tower bombings of the World Trade Center on September 11, 2001, are still fresh in the minds of many people. While still infrequent in the US, the numbers of such occurrences around the world have been on a steady rise over the course of the past decade or so.

Besides terrorist attacks, mass shootings have also become a phenomenon. They can be just as devastating as terrorist attacks and bombings, if not more. They may not claim as many lives as a bombing, but they are equally horrific and threatening.

They may even be more dangerous than terrorist attacks, because there are very few warning signs that they are about to occur. They are unpredictable. Often, they revolve around personal vendetta, or someone who has serious psychological problems that have few observable warning signs.

This makes it all the more important for you to be prepared and look for ways to protect yourself from such acts of terrorism. You need to be aware of your surroundings and know how to survive mass shootings and terrorist attacks so that you can escape unscathed.

Let's look at some of the different ways in which you can protect yourself and evade harm during such incidents.

Consider Surroundings and Circumstances

We'll be discussing several strategies for surviving acts of terrorism and mass shootings. But keep in mind that the strategies you should use largely depend on the circumstances as well as your surroundings.

For example, if you are in an open public space, you may find it difficult to hide if there are bombings or shootings. In

Terrorist attacks, both in the United States and abroad, have given us a glimpse of the dangerous world we live in.

such a scenario, you need to run. On the other hand, if you are in a closed space such as an office, and someone is spraying bullets at you, you have a much better chance of survival if you hide than if you run.

So make sure you always take into consideration the surroundings and circumstances. This will increase your chances of survival exponentially.

Take Action

If you find yourself in the middle of a terrorist attack or an incident of mass shooting, your first reaction may be that of disbelief. You may not be able to figure out what to do as your mind stops functioning completely. This will cause you to become a sitting duck. But remember, a stationary target is easier to hit.

Hence, avoid panicking, calm yourself, and think of ways in which you can change the situation for your survival. Scout your surroundings for ways that you can use to escape the scene or for items that you can use to fight back.

Regardless of what you do, do not stand or lie idly. Whether you decide to run, hide, or fight back, do so after careful consideration of your options. However, do something to protect yourself. You do not improve your chances of survival at all by doing nothing and simply waiting for law enforcement to arrive. Take some initiative and try to survive the event through action rather than inaction. This will go a long way in helping you to see another day.

Running Away

One of the first and most basic instincts during mass shootings is to freeze out of fear and panic. You may find it difficult to move. Or if you can move, your panic may cause you to run in any direction that may be open, without even considering if that direction would be safe for you or not. Then again, another basic instinct besides running is to hide behind some solid object in order to prevent the bullets from hitting you.

All of these instincts—freezing, running willy-nilly, or hiding—may be wrong for the situation.

Freezing out in the open might make you more of a target. Hiding may not work, because bullets might pierce the object you are hiding behind, unless you take shelter behind a steel wall. Moreover, when you are hiding, you become a stationary target, and sooner or later, the shooter might get around the obstacle and find you. Hence, hiding may not be the best idea unless you are already at a safe distance from the shooter. On the other hand, running toward an open direction may actually put you out in the open and make you more likely to be a target.

Instead, you need to stay calm and calculate the best route that will get you to safety. Consider every direction and option.

Mass shooters and terrorists usually do not have any specific people to target. They simply choose a location based on their agenda and with a large number of people present. Once they have done so, they simply attack and try to harm as many people as they can.

When they start their attack, you may notice them shooting mostly in one direction. As a result, running in another direction might be a good choice. Especially consider running out of the shooter's line of sight or behind the shooter's back. Get as far away from the scene as possible in that direction.

Moreover, when you are running, avoid doing so along a straight path. Try to move about as much as possible, as a moving target is difficult to hit. Try to calculate the safest route of escape, and move as quickly as you can. Once you are far away from the shooter, take cover and hide. Try to warn security personnel so that they can take some action and apprehend the shooter.

Hiding

Again, it depends on circumstances, but often running away is the best tactic. But if you find yourself amidst a mass shooting scene in a closed space such as a restaurant, a metro/subway station, or other locations that have limited exits, it may be difficult for you to run from the danger.

So if you are unable to run, hide.

If you can, hide behind solid objects. A sturdy table, the counter of a restaurant, a support pillar for the building, a wall, and other obstacles may be great spots where you can take shelter momentarily.

However, these may not eventually prove to be the safest spots in the long run. Once you have taken shelter momentarily, try to think of ways in which you can get away from the shooters permanently. Look for rooms where you can hide for longer periods or calculate routes to get away from the scene.

Hiding may seem cowardly, but every minute you delay a shooter increases your chances of survival.

Once you have been able to find such a room or a path, get away from the scene as quickly as possible. If you are entering a room, bolt the door. This will prevent the shooters from being able to access the room and harm you. You can also use heavy furniture such as a chair, a desk, a sofa, or even a cupboard to hold the door.

Once you have been able to lock yourself in a room, turn the lights off so that the shooter is unable to determine where you are. If the shooters are unable to see their target, they will find it difficult to harm you. With the lights on, they may be able to locate their target with the moving shadows.

You must remember that even a few minutes of delay for a shooter to carry out his agenda may be enough for the police to come to your aid. You must do everything within your control to delay the shooters finding you as long as possible. Every minute that you delay a shooter increases your chances of survival that much more.

Silence Your Cell Phone

While your cell phone may be indispensable in alerting outsiders, it can also make you more vulnerable, especially if you are hiding. As soon as possible, switch it to "Silent" or "Vibration" mode so that it does not cause any sound that can give your hiding spot away.

Also, be careful that the light of the phone doesn't give you away. Cover the screen with your hand or your shirt to keep it dim.

Alert Law Enforcement

Whenever you find yourself in the middle of a mass shooting or a terrorist attack, make every attempt to alert police or other security personnel.

Yes, I understand that many preppers are suspicious of the police. (More about surviving police encounters later.) But getting help and saving your life need to take priority over other considerations. And as a survival prepper with situational awareness, you are most likely in the best position to help the authorities in this situation.

You will be able to provide more details to the authorities, much more quickly than another person who does not have your situational awareness. Hence, look for ways to call and alert the dispatch center about your situation, so that they can take the necessary actions to apprehend the guilty and save your lives.

But do so very carefully and be smart about it, as well. There is no point in losing your life while trying to alert the authorities. Do not take a risk of exposure during your attempt to contact the authorities. Make the call yourself only if you feel that you can do so without exposing yourself to the attackers.

If speaking out loud for a phone call would be risky, you can use texting or social media posts to alert others to your plight, and have them call the authorities.

Also, some communities now have text-to-911. You can open your phone's messaging app and send a text with the number 911 in the "to:" field. Not all communities have text-to-911, though. Plus your text does not include location information. So it's better to make a voice call to 911 if you can do so safely.

Also, don't become so glued to calling or texting for help that you lose focus on the situation. Keep your situational awareness. Keep looking around and assessing changes in what is happening around you.

Calling by Landline

Landline phones may be a better option for calling for help

Although mobile phones can be used to call for help from almost anywhere, it becomes difficult for the authorities to locate your position in case you drop the device. In such cases, the dispatch center may not know the location to send security personnel to, at least not immediately. So a landline phone may prove to be a better option to call for help.

Even if you drop the landline phone in your attempt to get away from the shooter, the dispatch center can locate the address from the telephone records and dispatch security personnel accordingly. This will save a few seconds for you and increase your chances of survival by that extra few seconds.

Using a landline phone also helps you to keep your hiding location safe from the shooters, as these devices do not always have LED screens that light up when in use. Hence, shooters do not have anything to determine where to target in order to injure or hurt you.

Fighting Back

If you are unable to run or hide, fighting back may be the best option.

Sure, running and hiding can increase your chances of survival by a great margin. However, fighting back at times may be your only option. By fighting back, you not only prevent yourself and other people from being hurt, but you also might manage to stop the shooters from causing any further damage.

If you can, don't fight back alone. Try to gather a group of people who are at the scene and fight the shooters. Of course, there is every possibility that some of you may be injured or even killed, but having a group attack them does a lot to dampen the courage of the shooters and increases the chances of survival.

What you have to understand is that shooters are often cowardly people who use guns and other such weapons to terrorize unsuspecting people. Hence, it gives them great pleasure and enhances their courage to see people dying, or even running and hiding from them. However, when they see people fighting back, their motives and agenda take a huge blow.

After all, terrorism, by its very definition, is the act of striking or instilling terror among people. The basic motive of all terrorists, regardless of their agenda, is to instill terror in the hearts and minds of people. When they see people not fearing their acts of terror, their actions take a setback, and they are forced to look for new ways to terrorize you again. This is exactly the thing that you can exploit and take advantage of.

When you fight back, whether alone or in a group, you force the shooters and the terrorists to look for new ways to terrorize you. They may stop for a few minutes to figure out what to do next, and this short duration can help you to overcome them and protect yourself. You might have to take the risk of being injured during such an act, but it will certainly increase the chances of survival for you and the other people stuck in the middle of such acts of terrorism.

Anything Can Be a Weapon

When fighting back, use anything you have access to as a weapon.

If you find yourself in the middle of a mass shooting or a terrorist attack, scout your surroundings for any items you can use to protect yourself and inflict the maximum damage to the attackers. Try to find slightly heavy objects, as they can do some real harm, and use them to their maximum potential.

A folding chair, a landline phone, a laptop, a computer monitor, a lamp, a framed print on a wall, or a ceramic coffee mug can all be used to bludgeon an attacker. Liquids, such as a cup of coffee or a mug full of beer, can be tossed in their face. When you have to fight back, even a pen can be used as a weapon. Use any item you can get your hands on. Any item that you can use to attack and injure your attacker just may help you survive the attack.

Aim for These Body Parts

Attackers, mass shooters, and terrorists mostly use their eyes, hands, and legs to spot, find, shoot, and kill people. So if you have to fight back, go after these parts of the body.

Go for the eyes if possible. Throw that coffee or pop you have at their face. Scratch and claw if you can. Or go for the arms, especially the hands and wrists. Hit them with whatever you can pick up from your surroundings. Or go for the legs, especially the knees and feet. These are the most vulnerable areas. Hit, kick, and punch these areas if you can. Strikes to these areas can be very painful and cause immense pain to the attackers. Such pain may stop them from attacking you and force them to focus upon their own pain.

When Law Enforcement Arrive

When the police arrive, keep in mind that their first duty is to find and stop the active shooters or terrorists. They will be completely focused on getting to the attackers. They will shoot anyone who appears to be a threat to them or others, whether that person is actually a threat or not.

That's why you should not attempt to approach these first responders to the scene. As a matter of fact, you should not move at all. Only move upon their order. If you move prematurely, they may misidentify you as a threat and attempt to shoot you. Wait for them to issue orders and comply with their orders.

If you have information for them, do not approach them. Wait for them to approach you. They also will not stop to help victims. If you are injured, do not expect them to help you. Medical help will follow soon after.

Don't Be a Hero

Ultimately, through all of this, don't try to be a hero. Don't fight back if you can hide. Don't hide if you can run.

Your best bet is always escape. Escaping might seem cowardly, but it means you get to live another day and be there for the loved ones in your life. Escape means you can go for help, and that is much more effective than risking your life by taking on the attackers single-handedly.

Run if you can, hide if you can't run, and fight only if you must.

Surviving a Riot

RIOTS ARE BECOMING AN INCREASING PART OF THE AMERICAN landscape. These dangerous situations threaten the lives of everyone involved because the crowd mind is wild, illogical, and violent.

Unfortunately, when a riot breaks out, normal civilized and lawful behavior goes out the window. Even otherwise law-abiding people will do whatever they want, such as looting, setting fires, or attacking others, with wild abandon.

If you end up trapped in one of these situations, it can be very frightening and even deadly. Even if you have no intention of misbehaving, you can be swept up with the crowd and end up attacked, beaten, or even robbed. That's why it is important to understand how to prepare for and survive if you find yourself in this sort of situation.

Avoidance

Of course, the safest course here is not to go into situations where riots seem likely. It may be obvious, but ideological rallies, social demonstrations, and public events where alcohol or drugs are readily available tend to be volatile.

These days especially, I recommend avoiding all politically motivated gatherings, rallies, and demonstrations. It doesn't matter how strongly you believe in a cause, the safety of you and your family comes first. So, avoid these types of gatherings. Find other ways to support the causes you believe in—through donating money, creating blogs, making social media posts, doing phone solicitations, etc.—and leave these situations that have a high "riot potential" to others.

Identifying Threats

If you do find yourself in a public situation that seems like it is spiraling out of control, use your situational awareness skills. Identify people and groups who may be possible threats in the area.

Look for and avoid groups or individuals who are:

- Yelling or screaming at others
- Actively assaulting others
- Chanting violent slogans
- Carrying weapons or items that could be used as weapons (signs, sticks, torches, flags, etc.)
- Attacking law enforcement officials
- Threatening others with or without provocation
- Destroying buildings, public property, or the personal property of others
- Looting nearby businesses

Avoid these people, and avoid confronting them. When you identify individuals that are potential threats and are escalating the situation, use the same approach we mentioned in the last chapter—run away if you can, or hide if you can't.

Running Away

When a riot starts, you need to move out of the area quickly.

In riots, safety lies in the opposite direction of the rioters. But if you are in the physical middle of the riot, moving against the crowd is likely to end up with you getting injured or trampled.

Instead, start by working your way out of the middle and toward the edges of the crowd. Once you are at the edge, you can head in the opposite direction.

As you head out of the area, stay out of the sight of violent rioters by sticking to the shadows of alleyways and buildings. However, avoid going down a dead-end street, as you may end up trapped with no escape. Find quiet and safe areas that haven't yet been affected by the riot.

You may encounter violent rioters on the fringes of the riot. Avoid all interaction with them. Don't confront them or try to calm them down.

Hiding and Fighting

If you cannot escape completely, you may have to hide. Follow the instructions we gave in the last chapter for barricading yourself in and avoiding attracting attention.

Just as with mass shooting situations, you may at times need to fight, but you should only do so if necessary.

Avoid being the aggressor or attacking people unnecessarily. This action will only provoke more violence, making you less safe. Instead, only defend yourself when necessary as you move away from the riot. Follow our suggestions earlier for fighting if you have to.

As always, though, run away if you can, hide if you can't, and fight only if you must.

Avoiding Law Enforcement

In addition to avoiding rioters, you should also avoid any law enforcement in the area.

Keep in mind that crowd control and antiriot troops are designed to stop riots and restore peace quickly and efficiently. As a result, they don't have time to stop and assess whether or not you or your family are a danger. The officers assume anyone in a riot is a danger. Unfortunately, this means that the police may attack you, arrest you, and even charge you with being a rioter.

In fact, they are likely to use various weapons to take down the riot. In the beginning, nondeadly weapons such as tear gas,

The police are not your enemy during a riot, but you should avoid them.

mace, tasers, and billy clubs are likely to be used to stop a riot from spreading. As the situation escalates, law enforcement officials will then expand to a deadly weapon.

As a result, you need to stay out of their way and let them do what they have to do. They aren't necessarily your enemy in this situation, but they may hurt you in perceived self-defense. So if you see law enforcement officials in the area, don't rush to them thinking they will save you.

Avoid all politically motivated large gatherings. Find other ways to support the causes you believe in, and stay away from these high riot potential situations.

Surviving Police Encounters

AS POLICE FORCES ACROSS THE UNITED STATES OF AMERICA
continue to integrate military-grade weapons, vehicles, and
tactics into their daily routines, police encounters have become
increasingly dangerous.

Not all police officers are bad, of course, but the bad ones
can be extremely dangerous. The upgrade of police hardware
to military levels has emboldened these "bullies with a badge."

Of course, if you are stopped by the police, you have no
way of knowing what kind of officer you're dealing with—a
good apple or a bully. Since the rash of police controversies
over the past few years, tensions have heightened. Because of
the killings of civilians by police, even getting pulled over for a
traffic citation might induce more anxiety than it did in the
past. So, too, can getting stopped by the police when you're
walking down the street, leaving a store or a bar, or even standing in your driveway or on your porch.

The fact of the matter is this: police encounters can occur
anywhere, even inside your own home, even if you're
innocent.

We've all seen stories of police raiding the wrong house or
apartment. Some people online even pull pranks called "swat-
ting" in which they call in fake tips that lead entire SWAT teams
to the doors of innocent people.

Any of these situations can get dangerous if not handled properly. Not only do the police have laws and codes of conduct they're supposed to follow, you do, too. But even if you're not legally obligated to follow some of the rules, you should do so to ensure the safest and easiest interaction with police.

Remain Calm

The first thing you should do when you find yourself in an encounter with the police is to try to remain calm. Granted, this is easier said than done.

The key here is to at least pretend that you're calm. Think of it as playacting or performance art. If you behave in a jittery or skittish manner, if you stumble for words or stutter, if you take long pauses between words or sentences, you might appear suspicious to an officer.

On the other hand, you shouldn't play it too cool or friendly. Don't treat the officer like a friend you haven't seen in years. For all intents and purposes, this is a professional encounter, and you should treat it as such.

Use a Neutral Approach

A good rule of thumb is to treat an encounter with police as you might treat a run-in with upper management at work. Try to be respectful and, crucially, swallow your pride and your ego. No one likes a smart-ass, especially police officers. Few people like, or can tolerate, arrogance.

Even if it's difficult or doesn't come naturally to you, you must temper your pride and ego. Try to control outbursts. Keep a level tone when speaking with the officer. Try to use neutral language.

You should especially refrain from taking an adversarial,

"us versus them" approach. Your objective during any police encounter is to manage it smoothly. Unnecessarily provoking officers by acting aggressively or confrontationally could land you in jail—or on a slab at the morgue.

As we noted above, use neutral language. Don't poke fun at the officer or insult him or her. Try to speak as respectfully as the situation allows.

It's important to note, however, that you don't want to use certain words—such as "boss"—that might indicate you've served time. Even if you've never so much as received a parking ticket, the moment you create the impression that you've had previous run-ins with the law is a moment you'll regret. At the very least, this could prolong your confrontation. If the officer thinks you're a criminal, he or she might take their time to assess whether or not they've caught you in the middle of some kind of crime.

Minimize the Threat

Even if you experience genuine fear or anxiety during a police encounter, it should go without saying that you shouldn't run. Fleeing will guarantee an arrest, a warrant if you somehow manage to escape, jail time, or the worst case scenario: death. Although the urge to run might overwhelm you, even if you've done nothing wrong, you must resist it.

Coinciding with tempering your pride, you should follow any orders that an officer issues. If he or she tells you to step back or to stand on a curb or to lean against the squad car or a building, then you must do it. If they tell you to stop talking, listen. If they ask for your name, license, or ID, give it to them.

Yes, I understand that you may well be within your rights to deny their request.

Since the rash of police controversies over the past few years, tensions have heightened.

But your goal as a survival prepper is to end the interaction quickly and get back home to your family safely. Your goal is NOT to school the police in what is right and wrong, or to wind up as a martyr for a cause.

Interacting with Police

Minimize your interaction during the police stop as much as possible. Don't argue. Don't try to explain your situation, whatever it might be. Don't appear the least bit confrontational. Such behavior could raise red flags for the officers, something you must avoid. The less of a threat you appear to be, the better your chances of ending the encounter quickly.

You should also pay close attention to your arms and hands. Never put your hands in your front or back pockets. Don't speak with your hands. When you're talking to the officer, or listening, it's best to keep your arms at your sides. Make sure not to press them against your sides, however. Keep a gap between your arms and your body.

Also don't make any quick movements, especially with your hands. Don't reach for your ID—whether it's in your pocket or in the glove box of your car—until you are asked for it. Under no circumstances do you want to create the impression that you're reaching for something, or trying to grab or snatch something.

Patience Is Your Best Weapon

During the course of the interaction, preferably sooner than later, you should try to determine whether or not they're detaining you. How? By simply asking. Using neutral language, explicitly ask if they're detaining you. Again, set your ego aside. Don't say it in a way they might interpret as confrontational. Pose it as a genuine, honest question. "Officer, am I being detained?" If they say no, then ask, "Am I free to go?"

If they say you are being detained or that you are not free to go, then try to ascertain why they've stopped you. Again, refrain from being confrontational. If they tell you that you're not currently being detained but you're also not free to go at the moment, then you should try to remain as patient as possible. Repeatedly demanding to know whether or not you're being detained might frustrate, annoy, or even anger them—a recipe for a lengthy waste of time, or legitimate disaster.

As you may or may not know, police can stop you for a variety of reasons. At the very least, they must find something about your behavior suspicious or they must have probable cause that you've recently committed a crime or are in the process of committing a crime. Whether you have or not is irrelevant here. What's important is how you navigate the situation.

If they ask to search you or your vehicle, never consent to it. Unless they have reasonable cause to do so, police can't search your person or vehicle without either your explicit consent or a search warrant. Tell them in no uncertain terms that you do not consent to a search. Don't explain why. Don't attempt to justify your decision. Just tell them in response to any questions, "I do not consent to a search."

Remaining Silent

Other than asking, "Am I being detained, or am I free to go?" and other than saying, "I do not consent to a search," you should say little else. Especially avoid answering any questions. Remaining silent is often the best response.

Yes, it's difficult to be silent when police officers are talking to you, asking you questions, and especially if they are making accusations that you know are not true. It's also hard if they are threatening you with arrest or bodily harm. You'll want to argue back.

But don't. Again, patience is your strongest weapon in these encounters.

Also, don't try to "read" an officer—that is, to try to figure out what kind of person he or she is. You might possess impressive people skills, or abilities to manipulate others in your day-to-day life, but don't attempt any of that on cops. They deal with enough people every day, and with a large variety of personalities, that they've seen it all before. If they suspect you're manipulating them, it will create more problems.

By the way, make sure that your family and friends understand all of this.

Have discussions with them about how to behave during police encounters. Do this ahead of time. If you're out with friends, and you unexpectedly find yourself in a police encounter, you don't want a member of your group becoming cocky, mouthy, or violent. No matter how well you act, your friend or family member could cause a situation to go from bad to worse quickly for everyone involved.

Ending the Encounter

As soon as you are free to go, then go! Do not delay. Don't run or speed away, but move calmly and directly away from the encounter.

When the officer turns to leave, or tells you to leave, at the conclusion of an encounter, do it. Resist the urge to argue or get the last word in. Don't make smart remarks. Get out of there. You wouldn't want to reach the end of an encounter only to spoil and prolong it through your own behavior.

Besides awareness for events like mobs, mass shootings, and police encounters, there are other situations that may occur in your life. Some of these are "bigger" situations where you have little to no control.

A financial collapse would certainly fit into this category.

Surviving Financial Collapse

A FINANCIAL COLLAPSE OCCURS WHEN THE ECONOMY OF A nation, region, or territory breaks down. It's often preceded by an unrecoverable depression in the economy that lasts for months and years. It can also be caused by a run on money, where savings depositors and investors withdraw more funds than the economy can bear.

Economics and financial systems may be difficult subjects to understand, but the effects of a financial collapse are easily observed. Increasing prices, decreasing purchasing power, food shortages, power grid collapse, and scarce resources are all situations you may have to contend with. As the depression lingers on, side effects such as increased poverty and civil unrest can occur.

While we could write a whole book on how to survive a financial collapse, here are some key steps you can take to help you prepare.

Extending Your Hunkering-Down Plan

The best insurance for surviving a financial collapse, and for easing the transition to life afterward, is to extend your hunkering-down plan. Earlier, we advocated having a minimum of a 10-day kit of supplies. Extending this to a 30-day or 90-day kit means you will have time to adjust and adapt to the postcollapse world.

The same is true with your bug-out plan. If you can extend that plan to include multiple bug-out methods and multiple bug-out locations, you'll have more options for surviving the collapse.

Increasing prices and decreasing purchasing power may be signs of a financial collapse.

Prepare to Go "Off-Grid"

When I say the "grid," most people immediately think of the network of relays and stations that provides us with electric power. But the grid can also include other utilities such as natural gas and water that are delivered to your home. A more comprehensive view of the "grid" includes food distribution —the companies, transportation methods, and local markets that bring us our daily nourishment.

In a financial collapse, some or all parts of this extended grid may be disrupted. So it just makes sense to develop your own plan B for how to live and survive without relying on the grid.

Here are some examples of living off-grid. You can look at many of these ideas as exten-

Install a wind-and-solar generator to keep your house powered during a financial collapse.

sions to the hunkering-down and bug-out plans you've already begun developing:

- Dig your own well so you can have an independent water supply using the underground water table and deeper spring-fed water systems.
- Install solar panels and a wind turbine to generate independent sources of natural and existing energy from the sun's heat and the wind's force.
- Stockpile heirloom seeds and grains with your food rations, to plant your own garden and grow your own food. Study hydroponic (water-based, not soil-based) gardening, in case the soil in your area becomes unusable for growing.

- Stockpile firewood and a reliable source of tinder. Waterproof matches, tinder, and well-dried and cured firewood stockpiled in a dry, cool place will come in very handy in the first chaotic aftermath of the financial collapse.
- Assemble hunting gear. A reliable scope, a compass, a solar-powered flashlight, carving knives, and similar gear will make hunting for food much faster and easier after the financial collapse.
- Create a mobile base (such as a self-sustaining RV or campsite)—your own grid, in essence—that you can take with you as needed.

Bartering

Before there was today's near-total reliance on banking and credit, the mainstream economic system was one of barter.

One person had a chicken that laid eggs. The next person had a cow that generated milk. Still another person had a farm that grew produce. Each of these people could trade some of their bounty with their neighbors so all three people had reliable access to eggs, milk, and produce. This is a simplistic example, of course, but it worked beautifully for millennia until monetary currency and credit became the norm.

With a bit of planning and preparation, it can work beautifully again when credit is no longer an option to get basic human needs met.

Here, your goal is simply to decide what role to play in a barter-based economy. In other words, what will you have to offer?

Power could be a valuable commodity. If you have your own grid set up (solar and wind power, water well, etc.), that could be a means of barter to get other basic necessities. Being able to grow extra food or hunt extra animals that you could use for trade will also be a valuable skill. Raising animals would also be a valuable skill. You could keep goats or sheep, chickens or cows, horses or working dogs. That would be another strong source of barter on multiple levels.

You may also consider stockpiling items that could be used for barter.

Keep in mind, though, that items of great value now may have little to no value in a barter society. For instance, while a diamond ring might be worth thousands today, someone might consider a jug of clean water to be infinitely more valuable after a financial collapse.

Just about everything we include in our prepping plans will become valuable after an economic collapse. Consider storing extra quantities of every item on your hunkering-down list.

Beyond what is on our hunkering-down list, there are items that will have great value but aren't absolutely necessary for survival. This could include consumable items like alcohol, cigarettes, coffee and tea (especially the instant varieties), and chocolate.

Recreation items like playing cards, board games, and puzzle books may also become valuable. Actually, all types of books will be in demand, but especially reference books with information on how to live off the grid.

One good source of bartering may be personal hygiene items such as tampons and sanitary napkins. Even condoms may be in great demand. Ammunition may also be valuable.

Cash Reserves

It may seem like nonsense to keep cash on hand if a financial collapse occurs. But there will be a time early in the collapse when paper cash and coins may still have some value. That's because during the crisis, not everyone will accept that it is happening. They may not believe that the collapse will be total or permanent. So they may be willing to accept currency for food, water, and basic necessities.

You should plan for the safe and secure stockpiling of some currency. Use a fire-safe, water-safe storage box that is suitable for storing paper and coins. Make sure it is not too humid in the interior.

In addition, converting some paper currency to gold, silver, and other precious metals can further preserve your own cash reserves now and in preparation for use after a collapse. These metals have held their value for centuries and may become important in the postcollapse economy.

Self-Defense

In the wake of a financial collapse, expect rioting, looting, panic, widespread violence, and other "all for me, none for you" behaviors. People don't generally do well when all of a sudden everything that they have relied on is ripped away. This happens even when the deprivation is, to all intents and purposes, quite temporary. So imagine what kind of dangerous and even deadly behaviors might arise when the financial collapse is permanent.

Now is a good time to consider self-defense and family defense. Here are some ideas:

- Begin training in the art of self-defense. There are many options, from mixed martial arts to classic hand-to-hand combat techniques. Pick one and learn it very well.

- Select and learn to use firearms. We'll discuss this option in more detail later in this book, in the section on home security.
- If your state offers "concealed carry" certification, get it and carry your weapon. Since you don't know precisely when a financial collapse will occur, it is wise to be able to keep your weapon concealed with you at all times for your safety and your family's safety.
- Consider other sources of self-defense. If the collapse continues for a long time, bullets will eventually run out. Unless you have a plan to make your own ammunition (which is smart and entirely possible to put into place), you will need additional sources of self-defense. We'll discuss this later in the book, in the home security chapter on firearm alternatives.

A financial collapse is certainly one of those "big" situations we have no way of preventing. But there is another situation, one that has become more of a threat over the last few decades as we've become more reliant on technology.

And that is the cyberattack.

Surviving Cyberattacks

A CYBERATTACK IS ANY DELIBERATE DISRUPTION OF A COMPUTER system, a computer network, or a computer service. It can be as simple as attackers trying to steal your identity by planting spyware on your laptop computer. It can be as big and complicated as terrorists attempting to take down the entire World Wide Web.

As we become more reliant on technology in the digital age, the threat of a cyberattack has become more real and more frightening than it was even a few short years ago. Virtually every service and every method of communication now relies heavily on our ability to access the internet.

As a result, we have to prepare for a situation where we may be cut off from this technological resource.

Forewarned Is Forearmed

Of course, the first step in surviving a cyberattack is to learn how to prevent one from occurring in the first place. The western world is especially susceptible to the dangers posed by a terrorist cyberattack, and our enemies know this.

For example, just think about your job and the way in which you're paid. Most employers offer direct deposited pay, and, even if you don't participate, ask yourself when was the last time you dropped by an ATM. Speaking of your banking, your savings would likely be lost in the event of a significant cyberattack.

Another example? Most, if not all, public services are controlled via computers. This means there wouldn't be running water for showers, for toilets, or for drinking water. Likewise, gas pumps would no longer work for fueling automobiles, forcing everyone into a more pedestrian-based society.

Considering all the use of technology today, it wouldn't take long for our communities to devolve into barbarism and chaos. Without dropping a single bomb, a cyberattack can debilitate our communities within a very short span of time.

Much of the advice from the last chapter, on financial collapse, also applies to the results of a large-scale cyberattack. So let's start with more personal threats and concerns, and steps you can take now to protect yourself from more immediate attacks.

Protect Your Identity

Monitor your credit profile through semiannual reviews. This is one way of discovering if you've been a victim of identity theft or of a cyberattack on the businesses and financial institutions you rely on.

One way to minimize your exposure here is to use cash whenever possible for in-person transactions. This will give fewer businesses and institutions access to your financial information and provide fewer opportunities for your transactions to be monitored or your information to be stolen.

Get an RFID Blocker

It's very likely that your credit and debit cards now have RFID chips in them. While the chips allow for more secure transactions when you get to the checkout line of your local retail store, they also make you that much more susceptible to identity theft. Unless you keep your cards in a wallet or case equipped with an RFID blocker, anyone with a handheld scanner can access the information contained within the chips. They don't even need to take the cards out of your pocket or purse. They merely need to point the scanning device in your direction.

Don't Use Your Debit Card

Debit cards offer far less protection against hackers and identity thieves than credit cards.

Don't use your debit card for online or offline purchases.

Currently in the United States, under the Fair Credit Billing Act, your maximum loss on fraudulent credit card transactions is capped at $50, and many credit card companies will not charge you at all for transactions made on a stolen card number.

But you have no such protections on your debit card transactions. Under the current US Electronic Funds Transfer Act, if you fail to report your stolen card number within two days of it being stolen, you may be liable for up to $500 of the fraudulent activity. If you fail to report it within 60 days, you may be held responsible for all the transactions that have occurred.

As a result, your credit card is much safer for all transactions. Never use your debit card in restaurants, at stores, at gas stations, or online. Keep in mind that anyplace where your debit card leaves your sight puts you at risk. But even swiping the card yourself puts you at risk of "skimming"—where the swipe device has been altered by thieves to steal your number as you pay.

Protect Your Technology

If a widespread cyberattack occurs in your area or nationwide, and if doesn't disrupt power, you should immediately disconnect all of your computer devices from internet services. This includes tablets and mobile devices, as well as laptops and personal computers.

Next, run your antivirus software and scan for threats that may have already infected your devices. If scans do reveal a threat, the best course of action is to perform a system restore of the system or device to a period before the cyberattack occurred. Then, run the scan a second time to ensure the threats have been eliminated.

That means you should prepare ahead of time by having

up-to-date backups for all of your devices. Search online for automated services that back up your devices on a daily or weekly basis.

Prepare for Lengthy Power Outages

As previously mentioned, a cyberattack on a grand scale will almost certainly result in a massive and long-term power outage. How long? The United States and parts of Canada have already experienced accidental outages that have lasted from a day or two up to a week, so it's not inconceivable that an outage as a result of a cyberattack may last at least that long. A planned cyberattack that could accomplish a wide-scale power outage might also keep the power from being reinitialized quickly.

All of the planning we gave in the last chapter also applies to prolonged power outages:

- Extend your hunkering-down plan to cover 90 days.
- Make preparations to live off-grid.
- Keep some cash reserves, because you may no longer be able to use credit or debit cards.
- Stockpile items for barter with your neighbors and local shops.

Speaking of local shops, unless your local grocery stores have a contingency plan in place that allows them to operate without electricity, most grocery stores will be closed.

In that event, the next best option may be "dollar stores." As everything is the same price, store operators may allow cashiers to use handheld calculators to cash out customers. This is one way that stash of cash will come in handy.

Surviving EMP Strikes

AN ELECTROMAGNETIC PULSE (EMP) ATTACK IS SIMILAR TO A cyberattack, not in how it is accomplished, but certainly in what happens as a result.

An EMP is a powerful burst of electromagnetic energy. It can occur from the sun as a massive solar flare, from a lightning strike to power lines, or from a man-made attack using an EMP bomb or even a nuclear explosion.

This burst of energy will "fry" just about every electronic device you have in your home. It will also likely damage the entire electrical power grid, certainly in the area of the strike, and failures may cascade to the entire US power grid, or even grids in other countries.

The likelihood that the power would be working within a few days or weeks in a worldwide EMP phenomenon or a US EMP attack would be highly unlikely. Preparing for a large-scale EMP is the key to surviving one of these scenarios, because the government may not be prepared for this type of catastrophe.

Many of the preparations from our last two chapters on financial collapse and cyberattacks apply here. But let's focus on some more specific preparation you might need for an EMP attack.

Appliances and Devices

Consider that any household item that is not specifically shielded against EMPs will no longer work after an attack. This includes electronic devices like desktop computers, laptops, tablets, cell phones, telephones, internet routers, and televisions. But these days, even refrigerators, microwaves, ovens, thermostats, and even your toaster and coffee maker may have computer chips in them that will be fried. Just about any device that uses electricity may also be affected.

Don't think that your computer's surge protector will protect you. Household and office surge protectors are not strong enough to withstand an EMP. If you aren't near the main area

Not all threats are man-made. Even lightning can create a devastating EMP strike.

of attack and are more on the fringes of the actual event, they may possibly help, but don't rely on them.

Public and Private Infrastructure

Besides the power grid, many other parts of the public and private infrastructure will be affected. This includes other utilities (gas, water), banking systems, traffic lights, public transportation, air traffic control, and hospital equipment. Expect there to be little to no service in these areas.

Once again, you can see the importance of having at least a 90-day hunkering-down kit to see you through this time.

Personal Transportation

Note that bugging out by vehicle will most likely be impossible.

Most modern automobiles are computer-controlled. An EMP may wind up damaging your car's internal circuitry beyond repair. More than likely, your car will no longer start or run. Actually, this may be your first clue that it is an EMP attack, and not just a simple power outage due to grid failure or cyberattack.

You may want to include nonmotorized transportation, such as bicycles, skateboards, and rollerblades, with your hunker-down supplies. These can be used if you do need to bug out, but they'll have a practical use even if you are hunkering down. Immediately after the EMP event, you can use these to get to your child's school to pick her or him up, and to get around town to help other family members and friends.

Many of your bug-out supplies, such as a bug-out bag, walking shoes, etc., may come in handy after an EMP event. You may not actually bug out, but you might use them for getting around should you need to venture out after the attack.

Away from Home

Speaking of disabling your car, keep in mind that you may actually be in your car or away from home when the EMP hits. Because of that, you should have, at a minimum, food and the appropriate clothing for an emergency in your car at all times. In order to get back home, you may need to walk, so always carry comfortable shoes and socks in your car. If you have a bigger vehicle, such as an SUV, a fold-up bike that you keep in there at all times would be ideal.

It is important to have a flashlight in the car at all times, as well. In case of an EMP at night, it will be necessary to bring it with you as you find your way home.

Blankets should be kept in the car for cold weather emergencies, and just in case you need to stay the night in the car or elsewhere.

Protection should be considered. A firearm in your vehicle may also be helpful. Check the laws in your state to make sure you comply with how to transport firearms. (We'll cover more about firearms and firearm alternatives later in the book, in our section on home security.) A hunting or survival knife kept in your car can also be used as a weapon.

Surviving Extreme Weather Conditions

THE SITUATIONS WE'VE LOOKED AT SO FAR IN THIS SECTION HAVE been man-made events over which we have little control: riots, mass shootings, cyberattacks, financial collapse, and EMP attacks.

But let's consider two more events that are less man-made and more natural in origin. These are the weather conditions of extreme heat and extreme cold.

Extreme Heat

Every year, deaths occur from hot weather conditions. But many of these deaths are avoidable. By learning how to survive in sweltering environments, you'll stand a better chance of overcoming the destructive impacts of high temperatures.

Before preparing to survive in hot weather conditions, it makes sense to fully appreciate the very real risks imposed by heat. What happens when ambient temperatures soar? Why does this situation become life-threatening?

Remember, the human body is a remarkable living organism. Your organs consist of millions upon millions of tiny cells functioning together in unison. Most systems in the body operate dependably without requiring conscious direction.

You don't need to instruct your heart to beat or your blood to circulate, for instance. These functions occur automatically in the background.

A variety of cellular messengers within the body called "enzymes" help regulate all this complex cellular activity. Unfortunately, as temperatures rise, many enzymes stop working correctly. In fact, high heat may cause some of them to literally unravel.

What does this situation mean for human beings (and their pets) exposed to high temperatures?

Someone exposed to a heat wave may quickly become dehydrated and disoriented. Muscles may begin cramping, and the person may feel nausea. Hot weather also aggravates some preexisting medical conditions. It frequently causes heat exhaustion, a condition in which the body must work harder simply to survive. People with heat exhaustion may develop "heat stroke," an exceedingly dire situation in which cells begin losing the ability to maintain normal physiological processes.

Heat stroke may produce deadly changes in the body. This condition requires immediate medical attention. But there is a lot you can do beforehand to prevent this condition from even happening.

Prepping for Extreme Heat

To protect your entire household during hot weather, keep these points in mind:

- Consider the comfort and needs of everyone in your household on an individual basis.
- Remember that hot weather may aggravate preexisting medical conditions.

- The very young and seniors typically prove more susceptible to the impacts of high temperatures than healthy young adults, but everyone is vulnerable.
- Remember to include pets in your hot weather planning. They can suffer heat stroke, too.
- Depending on the ambient temperature, air conditioning becomes essential in order for some individuals to survive a heat wave without encountering medical problems.
- In some locations, the impact of large numbers of people using electricity during a heat wave stresses power grids, so power failures may occur unexpectedly.
- Installing a backup generator to ensure that your home enjoy uninterrupted electricity could enable you to continue operating an air-conditioning system during a power failure.
- Drink water to remain well hydrated during hot weather and avoid alcoholic beverages (alcohol dehydrates the body).
- Prepare your vehicle for hot weather conditions by keeping your car well maintained to reduce the chance of breakdowns. Carry a supply of drinking water, a tarp for shade, and a cell phone (to summon emergency assistance) in your car.
- Draw up a hot weather plan for all your animals, as well. You may need to consider bringing outdoor pets into air-conditioned locations during heat waves to avoid pet health problems.

Your local area will likely influence your hot weather plan. For instance, some cities offer emergency hot weather shelters with available air conditioning to assist residents during heat waves. In these locations, if a power failure occurs, sending your family to an emergency shelter provides a very cost-effective solution. (However, you'll want to check in advance to make certain you can rely on this option.)

Additionally, remember many public buildings such as courthouses, airports, and shopping malls include generator systems to help keep air conditioning operating during a power outage. If your community lacks a hot weather shelter, relocating to these sites during the hottest periods of the day may help prevent heat-related health emergencies.

Daily Preparation for Extreme Heat

You'll want to monitor weather forecasts during the hottest months of the year in your area. Use a weather app on your smartphone and set it up to provide you with weather alerts.

Try to schedule your daily activities with temperature issues in mind. Dressing in reflective light-colored clothing and wearing a hat with a wide brim or a sun visor will help you feel cooler on hot days.

Always carry water along with you during outdoor exercise in the summer. Dehydration occurs very quickly in hot weather.

Taking Soaring Temperatures Seriously

In recent years, tragic deaths have occurred when people exercised on running trails or hiking trails during heat waves. Remember even if you are a robust, healthy individual, you can still get heat stroke. Limit your outdoor activity during extreme hot weather.

If you do find yourself outdoors feeling overwhelmed by

the heat, request emergency assistance quickly. Try to wait for help to arrive in a shaded location, if possible.

Extreme Cold

Extreme cold affects the human body in a different way from the way extreme heat does. In cold conditions, the body takes steps to protect your most vital organs such as your heart, lungs, and kidneys. It will

Limit your outdoor activity during extreme heat conditions.

divert most or all of the blood supply to keep these organs functioning. That means it will move blood away from the extremities.

The reduced blood flow to the skin increases the risk of frostbite on exposed areas of the skin. Even the eyes may freeze with prolonged exposure.

With the lack of blood flow to the arms and legs, people begin to feel slow and lethargic. With further exposure, their body temperature and metabolism will drop, making them feel mentally disoriented, as well. Eventually, their body will begin to shut down. They'll experience breathing problems, uncontrollable shivering, fatigue, slurred speech, and poor coordination.

All of this adds up to a state of sluggishness, making their situation more life-threatening. Their thought process and judgment will be impaired. Their breathing may then begin to slow down, depriving their bodies and brains of oxygen.

At this point, it's not unusual for people to become so dis-oriented that they begin to remove their clothes. They feel like they are too hot—actually burning up—but in reality, they are continuing to lose body heat. Undressing just accelerates the process and brings them that much closer to death.

Prepping for Extreme Cold

Just like with extreme heat, you'll need to consider each person in your family and what they'll need to deal with the cold. Cold can aggravate some medical conditions, and the very young and seniors are the most vulnerable. Some pets often can handle extreme cold better than extreme heat, but they are still vulnerable. You may need to bring them inside as well to help them keep warm.

In extreme cold, access to a heat source, such as the central heating in your home, is important. Keep in mind, though, that large numbers of people using gas or electric central heating puts stress on the utility grid. Having a backup method of heating your home is necessary. This could be a fireplace, a wood-burning stove, or a backup generator and portable electric space heaters you can plug into it.

Make sure you maintain your vehicles and prep them for cold weather conditions. Carry blankets, additional clothing, food and water, and a cell phone for just such emergencies.

Daily Preparation for Extreme Cold

If you need to venture outside in extreme cold, dress warmly and keep as much of your skin covered as possible.

You may have heard of "dressing in layers." That means avoiding big heavy clothing that make movement difficult and become uncomfortable as you sweat. Instead, dress in smaller thin layers that help the body stay warm.

Specifically, you'll want three layers of clothing.

First is a base layer next to your skin. This layer should wick away perspiration from your skin to keep you dry and to retain heat. That will help prevent hypothermia. Cotton, used in many undergarments, is a poor choice. Synthetic fabrics such as polyesters are ideal for this layer. Look for briefs, bras, long underwear, t-shirts, and tights made for this purpose.

The second layer is an insulating layer. This layer is designed to protect you from the cold. Specifically, the clothing should trap air next to your body, which warms, keeping you warm. Wool and fleece are ideal for this layer.

The third layer should be a shell layer. This layer is designed to protect you from atmospheric moisture—snow or rain—and

If you need to venture outside in extreme cold, dress in layers to minimize exposure.

from wind. This should be made of waterproof or water-resistant fabric but should ideally be "breathable" to allow the venting of moisture away from the body. Again, synthetic fabrics are ideal for this layer. Most of this clothing is specifically identified as "rainwear" or "mountaineering wear."

Take Falling Temperatures Seriously

Venturing out in extreme cold is risky. Avoid leaving home and driving in extremely cold weather. Don't head out in the middle of a snowstorm. Wait for the weather to improve.

If you do drive out and happen to get stuck, the best thing to do is stay with your car. Do not head out on foot looking for help. The only exception here is if there are buildings close by. A building may provide better shelter. But in the absence of buildings, stay with your car.

If your car still runs, you can periodically turn it on to keep yourself warm and then turn it off to conserve fuel. But make sure your exhaust system and tailpipe are clear of snow, to prevent deadly carbon monoxide fumes from building up. Check your tailpipe before each time you start the car. If you don't have a digging tool to clear the snow, use the tire iron from your trunk.

Staying hydrated is important, even in the cold. If you don't have water, you can melt snow and drink it. Allow it to melt first, if possible. The snow can also be eaten in small amounts to give you enough water to survive. But since the snow is cold, the body will have to expend extra energy to warm it up. So the more snow you eat, the more calories you will burn. The body will already be burning a lot of calories to try to keep you warm. Eating snow causes further temperature drops. So allowing the snow to melt and drinking it will help stave off extra energy loss.

Wrap yourself up in blankets to help hold in the heat. If you don't have blankets, cut into the material of your car seats. The foam underneath the seat cover makes good insulation. Wrap it on top of shoes, clothing, and exposed skin to prevent frostbite. Use nonessential wires ripped out of the car to tie it in place.

Exercising and movement can help keep you warm, even if you are trapped in the car. Move your legs and arms periodically. If you need to sleep in your car, it is far better to sleep during the day than at night. The daytime will be frigid, but warmer, so you are at greater risk at night. Night is the better time to turn on the car periodically, to eat and drink, and to exercise to keep you warm.

Prep your vehicles for cold weather conditions, and carry blankets, additional clothing, food and water, and a cell phone.

PART 5

Home Security and Weapons

Securing Your Home

HOME SECURITY AND CRIME PREVENTION ARE HOT TOPICS—EVEN without adding an extreme event to the mix. While there are steps you can take to keep your family and property safe every day, securing your home during disasters and times of upheaval takes another level of care.

These steps will help prevent physical injury from criminals who would do you harm during uncertain times. They also make sure all the carefully chosen and stored supplies you gathered remain under your ownership.

Securing Your Home and Property

Understanding the enemy is a big step toward being able to stop him. Look over your house with a "burglar's eye" and identify any weaknesses that would allow someone to enter your home unwanted.

Know that while a seasoned sneak thief may target homes based on the probability of wealth inside, the average looter or desperate person looking for food or guns is always going to go for a "softer" target.

Making your home and your family look more "difficult" will deter these people.

During an extreme event, a professionally installed electronic home security system offers some level of deterrence, as

A "No Trespassing" sign shows you'll defend your property with force and may make criminals think twice.

long as the electricity is still on. With clearly displayed signs indicating the presence of a security system, some criminals may bypass your home and move on to pick an easier target.

But in the case of a disaster or a breakdown in normal society, there's a good chance that the electricity will be intermittent at best. Your expensive alarms will be rendered useless.

Luckily, there are other ways to physically protect your property and set up barriers that will stop most people intent on stealing from you or harming you.

The sign for your security system, even if the system itself is inoperable, may still make criminals think twice. But the addition of other signs may also act as a deterrent. These include "No Trespassing" and especially "Beware of Dog." "No Trespassing" may indicate that you are willing to defend your property with force and may make criminals think twice. "Beware of Dog" is also a great deterrent. Hang this sign whether you actually have a dog or not.

In the event of a pandemic, a "Biohazard" sign hung prominently on the house may stop the bad guys, as well. Like the "Beware of Dog" sign, you can hang this sign whether you actually have the pandemic in your home or not.

Doors and Windows

We talked about fortifying doors and windows earlier, in the Hunkering Down part of this book. But let's focus on them now from a security perspective.

Upgrade your locks and strike plates to make it more difficult for miscreants to kick in the door.

First, make sure you have the right type of doors and windows installed. If necessary, upgrade the deadbolt lock and the strike plates for the locks on your front door. That will make it more difficult for miscreants to kick in the door.

The back sliding glass door is quick work to a hammer or rock, and the garage door can be kicked in without much trouble. Of course, glass windows are relatively easy to break. Steel-reinforced doors with sufficient deadbolts and multipane windows can help.

Keep doors and windows locked at all times and check them frequently. Also, use strong bars to prevent windows from sliding up or down, and door stoppers or door jams on the inside of doors so that they cannot be opened. Bulletproof glass is expensive, but there are adhesive films on the market that can provide some protection for much less. Even adding chicken wire across the inside can help stop breakage from thrown rocks and bottles.

Perimeter Protection

If electricity still works, regular or motion sensor lights can scare away thieves or alert you to their presence. It is possible to get alarms for gates, as well. If you want an even higher level of protection and if it's legal in your area, installing an electric fence is an option. However, if the electrical grid goes down, the fence won't be electrified, so only physical barriers will be useful.

A tall fence may deter thieves from breaching your property and instead encourage them to go looking for easier pickings elsewhere. Lock all gates with heavy-duty chains and locks that can't be undone through a gap or over the top of the fence. The best fences surround the perimeter of the property completely, either at the edge of the property or a distance away from the house.

Note that local laws sometimes restrict fence placement. You may also not be able to have a fence or gate across your driveway. In that case, add some "spike strips" to your hunkering-down supplies and deploy them in your driveway during the event.

Spike strips, however, can be expensive. A cheaper alternative, especially for smaller driveways, are caltrop spikes. Look online for caltrops that are specifically designed to puncture and flatten tires. Other cheaper alternatives are to throw a bed of nails or broken glass across the driveway. You can also do this around the entrances to your home to deter thieves on foot.

During emergencies, add razor wire or barbed wire to your fence or on the ground just inside of it.

In an acute situation where the criminal element is high and your property is under additional threat, add an extra "layer" to the inside of your fence. Place a smaller fence or even a stack of boards just inside your fence and top it with razor wire or barbed wire. Or if push comes to shove, just lay the wire on the ground inside your fence. If someone attempts to come over the top of your main fence, make it obvious that they will have a difficult landing inside the fence.

Personal Defense Options

For personal defense options, we're going to consider firearms and firearm alternatives in the next chapters. So for now, let's focus on other means of defense.

If someone does breach your property, you will need to defend yourself. Classes in basic self-defense are always a great idea for just about anyone who is concerned with safety. The training in these classes goes beyond the physical. They often help you develop the mental and emotional readiness to defend yourself. These are useful skills not just for emergencies and home invasions, but for everyday life, especially if you are away from home. Consider involving the whole family. Even children can learn some basics that may get them out of a tight spot.

Despite even the most stringent home security preparations, someone may get inside your home. One way to keep your family safe is to have a high-quality safe room built into your home. These can be purchased and installed either in something like a large walk-in closet, down in the basement, or even as a separate bunker on the property.

Another option is to simply take a place in your house—a room or a large closet—and reinforce it. It is easier to defend and protect a small space in your home than the entire house with multiple entrances. Install an exterior door and door frame, reinforce the walls, and stock the space with a charged phone, fresh water, some food, first aid supplies, and weapons.

Security Protocols

Physical barriers help prevent crime, and safe rooms and weapons may keep you safe. But very little of it will do much good unless you and your family are mentally prepared for their use.

Practice and be prepared to take action when that time comes. The entire family should practice security drills regularly so everyone knows exactly what to do in the case of an emergency. Assign jobs to everyone so that everything gets done quickly and nothing is forgotten. For example, while mom moves the emergency food cache to the secure room, dad barricades all of the doors. Children who are old enough should have jobs of their own. Not only will it help you get everything done when time is critical, it can also help the children from being overwhelmed with fear.

Speaking of everyone having jobs, it's important during these times to have a recognized "chain of command," along with the entire family's agreement to follow commands during a security emergency. A lot of confusion can occur if there are too many generals making conflicting decisions and not enough privates actually doing the work to keep the family safe.

One family member should be designated as the leader. The leader should not necessarily be the person most skilled or with the most knowledge about security, thought it may be. More important, the leader should be the person who can remain the most even-tempered and least panicked during a crisis. Even if this person is less skilled in prepping or in security, she or he will be better able to make calm decisions and delegate tasks to those in the family who do have the skills. The leader should be someone whom everyone in the family agrees to follow without question in an emergency.

Once you have a leader, that person should then decide on her or his chain of command—that is, who is next in charge should the leader not be able to function, who is after that person, and who is after that, on down the line.

This may be one of the most important family preparations you can do for security.

Camouflage Options

Not only will criminals bypass a property that looks difficult to get into or unsafe in favor of an easier target, they will also skip a house that looks like it has already been looted, damaged, or claimed by someone else as their party spot or gang hangout.

Use this knowledge to your benefit by camouflaging your home and property so it does not look appealing to people who want to steal stuff.

This does not mean you should break your own windows or set fire to your front porch. You want your home and yard to be in good condition when or if the world returns to normalcy again. You also do not want to damage anything that will keep someone or bad weather out.

But consider strewing trash, crumpled paper, empty bottles, and cans around outside to make it look like someone was hanging out there and everything good is gone. Spray paint a wall or two with graffiti to do the same.

Make it look like you have a huge, vicious dog or two by attaching a weathered chair to a tree next to a large water dish and maybe an old bone or chew toy. The people who live nearby won't be fooled, but a passerby might think twice.

Secrecy

Do not brag to strangers or casual acquaintances about your hunkering-down plans, your security methods, your weapons, or your supplies. The more people you tell about your plans, the more potential problems you invite should a security emergency arise. The fewer outsiders who know what you have, the safer you will be.

When things look their worst, some people will band together and have one another's backs. But far more will do anything it takes to preserve themselves and their families. So during these times, form alliances carefully, especially with neighbors. Even your friendly neighbor may turn on you when faced with hunger or violence that he is not prepared to deal with himself.

Also, if you leave your property, either to fetch supplies or check on what is happening nearby to judge safety levels, do so discreetly. Try to make sure your coming and going is unnoticed by others. If someone suspects you have weapons, fresh water, and food inside that they want, they may watch your property to see when it is unguarded. The last thing you want is to come home from a fact-finding mission to find someone broke into your home, looted it, and hurt the other members of your family.

Choosing a Defensive Firearm

SOME NEW SURVIVAL PREPPERS ARE LEERY OF GUNS. MANY HAVE never considered owning firearms, and they or their family members may not be supportive of storing firearms for self-defense.

If you are strongly antigun, I'm not going to try to convince you that you need a firearm. But I will say that you do need to consider some form of self-defense. During an emergency— whether you are hunkering down, bugging out, or sealing in— you may have to protect yourself and your family from those who would hurt or kill you to take your supplies.

Yes, there are risks to owning and using firearms. But when it comes to defending yourself from those who would harm you or your family, firearms are at the top of the list as far as versatility and effectiveness go.

If you are completely opposed to owning a firearm, please skip this chapter and move on to the next one on firearm alternatives.

However, if gun ownership is within your comfort zone, let's discuss some options.

The Best Gun to Own

You'll find a great variety of discussions—and quite a few dis-agreements and arguments—about the best gun to own for self-defense and for survival prepping. I have my own thoughts about this subject, which I'll tell you about in a moment.

But let me give you an overall rule of thumb:

The best gun to own is one that you are actually willing to use if your back is against the wall.

The best gun is one with which you are completely com-fortable, skilled, and well-practiced. So when we talk about long guns versus handguns, revolvers versus semiauto pistols, or rifles versus shotguns, we're really debating nuances. One

The shotgun has been called "the home invader's nightmare," but is it the best choice for defense?

firearm or another may have advantages in one situation and disadvantages in another. But you make the disadvantages even greater if you are not comfortable with, not skilled with, or not well practiced with your firearm.

So if you already have a firearm you are comfortable with, use it.

Having said that, though, here are some other considerations you might want to explore.

Long Gun or Handgun: Which Is More Effective?

An interesting trend has shown up recently. Of all the many types of ammunition available, there is a definite lean toward the purchase of rifle ammo. It would appear that rifles are becoming the weapon of choice for many people.

This makes sense, since rifles have much better stopping power than handguns. However, handguns may be more practical than rifles in certain cases.

One example is home defense. Although most people say they prefer a shotgun for its unrivaled stopping power, they usually change their minds after thinking about what it would take to defend and protect your family should intruders breach your home.

For example, to prevent revealing your position or having your gun taken from you while moving through your home, the end of your barrel should not precede you through a doorway or around a corner. So your long gun must be lowered or raised to keep it hidden from intruders.

In tense situations, you might need to guide and direct those depending on you for protection to your safe room. You may need to operate door handles and light switches along the way. To do so, you may need to control and operate your long gun with a single hand.

Both shotguns and rifles are two-handed weapons. Because of the length and weight of long guns, it is not easy for most people to maneuver them or fire them with one hand. It is especially difficult to acquire a target quickly from a raised or lowered position with only one hand.

Also, to intruders, the presence of a long gun may be reason for them to shoot at you immediately in order to prevent you from raising the weapon and shooting first.

A handgun would eliminate all of these possibilities.

In addition, long guns are also virtually impossible to conceal. In situations where you're not in a full-blown extreme event—that is, where there is still some rule of law—you may want to leave your home. You'll need to carry a weapon with you at those times. But you'll want to conceal it, so as not to draw attention to yourself and become targeted by criminals for the sole purpose of taking it away from you. Long guns won't work for that purpose.

Handguns are the most practical solution to many common defense situations you may find yourself in.

Although handguns are the practical choice in most situations, long guns do have their own place. In certain invasion situations, you would usher your family into a previously selected "safe room" in your house while carrying your handgun as your weapon. Ideally, your safe room would then be stocked with additional ammo and long guns. You could then use the long guns to defend your family against anyone who tried to breach the safe room.

Also for defense against a mob, a rifle or a shotgun would be better to use than a hand gun. Moving beyond defense to other survival uses, there are few substitutes that work as well as a long gun for hunting. So long guns do have a place in your home arsenal.

The Pros and Cons of Various Firearms

If you are still on the fence about which firearm you should purchase, here is a list of the pros and cons of the different types:

Revolvers

Pros:

- Easy to conceal
- Casings are retained and can be reloaded
- Long-barreled models can be used for shooting at greater distances
- Easy for novice shooters to use

Cons:

- Slower to reload than other guns
- Low ammunition capacity

Semiautomatic Pistols

Pros:

- Very easy to conceal
- Fast reload times
- Easily customizable
- High-capacity magazines available

Cons:

- Ammunition choices can be hard to find
- Long-range shooting not a strong point

Rifles/Carbines
Pros:

- Excellent for long-range shooting
- Have plenty of power, even with midrange cartridges
- High accuracy

Cons:

- Unable to conceal on your person
- Unable to carry without attracting attention
- Bulky and heavy ammunition

Shotguns
Pros:

- "The home invader's nightmare"—devastating stopping power at close range
- Can be used for small and large game
- Usually cheaper than pistols

Cons:

- Shorter range compared to rifles and carbines
- Heavy ammunition

If at all possible, consider purchasing a complete arsenal of firearms. This should include a shotgun, a semiautomatic rifle (e.g., an AR-15 or an AK-47), a full-size pistol, a long-range rifle (400 yards or farther) and a small-game rifle (.22 caliber).

In a pinch, you could use your semiautomatic rifle as a long-range gun with the proper ammunition. Small game can also be shot with a revolver or a pistol. But having a complete arsenal gives you options. It will enable you to handle just about any self-defense or home protection situation.

Also, firearms do not usually lose value and tend to appreciate instead. So should you later decide to upgrade your arsenal, you can often sell your older weapons. (Check your state and local laws on private gun sales.)

How and Where to Purchase a Firearm

Unless you really know the person who is selling you a used firearm or you are a firearms expert yourself, always buy a brand-new product.

Unscrupulous dealers plague the firearms market like anywhere else, and they would be more than happy to sell you something with flaws unnoticeable to the untrained eye. Also, most new firearms come with a manufacturer's warranty. That

While rifles and shotguns are popular, a handgun is more practical, especially indoors.

way, if anything goes wrong, you can have it repaired at minimal or no cost.

Stick with common calibers when purchasing your firearm. Specialty calibers such as .44 Magnum Special are hard to find and expensive to purchase.

Common calibers such as .223/5.56, .30–06, and .308 for rifles are easy to find. Common handgun calibers include 9mm, .45 APC, and .357.

When it comes to firearms and calibers, it all boils down to what you are most comfortable using. Under the right conditions, a .22 caliber bullet can be just a deadly as a .44 magnum load.

Training

Simply buying a firearm won't make you any safer. If you are unskilled with it, you may actually increase the risks to yourself and your family instead of protecting you and them.

Whatever firearms you choose, make sure you and your family are well trained with them. If you are inexperienced, get training. Search online for "firearms training" in your local area. Look for classes in gun safety, shooting, and personal protection. Make sure every member of your family is well trained.

Even if you never experience a disaster in your lifetime, owning firearms can provide you with peace of mind knowing that you can protect your family.

Four Alternatives to Firearms

ADAPTABILITY IS ONE OF THE MOST IMPORTANT SKILLS FOR survivalists and preppers. When it comes to personal defense, it's not enough to be skilled with firearms. Whether due to lack of ammunition, lack of firearms themselves, or the need for a quieter weapon, some situations may call for weapons other than your trusty handgun or long gun.

Here are some of the most effective alternatives:

Edged Weapons

Edged weapon are valuable for both survival and combat situations.

We can't emphasize enough the value of having a good knife, or several good knives, with your hunkering-down and bug-out supplies. A good knife can be used both as a skinning tool while hunting for food, as well a tool to fend off those who would take what you own.

At a minimum, I recommend you own two knives for survival purposes. One should be a smaller folding knife or pocket knife, and the other should be a medium-to-large hunting or survival knife.

Smaller knives can be carried inconspicuously in your

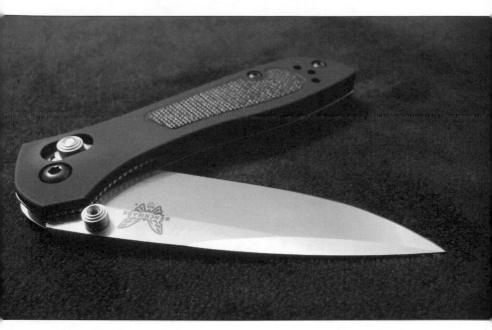

A smaller folding knife can be carried inconspicuously in your pocket.

pocket. They can also often be concealed in your hand, allowing for stealthy use before targets even know that they are being attacked.

For everyday carry in my pocket, I use a 4.5-inch folding knife with a locking 3.25-inch blade that has a plain edge. It's thin, which when folded makes it easy to carry and conceal on my person. But when opened, the steel is heavy-duty enough for basic use and for self-defense in up-close situations. Plus it has grip inlays to keep it from slipping should it or my hand get wet.

Note: Some states and cities limit which types of knives or which blade lengths can be carried in a concealed manner. Please check the laws in your area to see what is allowed.

As a second knife, I recommend a hunting or survival knife

that has a fixed, full-tang blade. Many of these knives will be plain-edged on one side of the blade and serrated on the other. The plain edge is good for straight cutting and self-defense, while the serrated edge is good for sawing through rope, material, small tree branches, etc. Look for a knife with an overall length of seven to 12 inches, with a blade length from four to seven inches.

Of course, you can include numerous other knives with your hunkering-down supplies or bug-out bag. A pocket utility knife (the kind that has a razor blade as an edge) is very handy and, if push comes to shove, can be pressed into service for

A hunting or survival knife has many practical uses, including self-defense.

self-defense. A set of kitchen knives—with a butcher's knife, carving knife, and serrated knife—isn't practical for bugging out but might come in handy at home when you are hunkering down, both for cooking and for combat.

Speaking of bug-out bags, I would include a small folding knife, a longer hunting or survival knife, and optionally a utility knife in each person's bug-out bag, with the exception of young children, who may hurt themselves on them. Having knives in each bag will make sure you have plenty of backup blades, should any break or become dulled.

You should also keep in mind that there are plenty of other edged weapons that you can use other than a knife. A good alternative is a good-quality hatchet or axe. Like the knife, hatchets and axes have multiple uses. An axe can help you gather firewood and other supplies and also serve as an incredibly intimidating weapon if the situation calls for it.

You can get small camping or survival axes about 14 inches in length that would be easy to carry with your bug-out bag. You may also want a bigger wood-chopping axe (36 inches or so). While too large to carry if you bug out on foot, it may come in handy with your vehicle bug-out kit or your hunkering-down supplies.

In between knives and axes are machetes. For something heavier than a knife but a bit lighter than an axe, get a machete in the 21-inch range. These actually make great weapons, because they allow you to strike from a greater distance than a knife, but they are easier to handle than a heavier axe.

Blunt Instruments

While blunt objects are a much less obvious choice for a weapon, there is no doubt that they can be effective in many situations, especially if you are ever attacked by another human.

Hammers make great, all-purpose blunt weapons. Not only can the hammer be used for building structures and tools, but it is also easy to use the hammer for aiming at certain body parts of your assailant during combat. A quick strike to the skull or kneecaps can certainly change the mind of an attacker who has decided to confront you. If you have the strength, you can also try a similar strategy with a sledgehammer for a more intimidating effect.

You can easily include these with your hunkering-down and vehicle bug-out supplies.

If you are hunkering down and your home is breached, you can improvise blunt instruments. Any large or heavy household object can probably be used as a weapon to some effect. In fact, you can easily use furniture, like a chair or a lamp, to fend off an attacking human or animal. A baseball or softball bat is also useful.

Items from your toolbox make great blunt weapons.

In addition to this, many items in a well-stocked toolbox can be used as weapons. For example, a well-made heavy pipe wrench can really make a difference if you are caught in a situation without a normal weapon.

You can also create a blunt weapon that is very intimidating. If you have a large stick, baseball bat, or a club-like implement, you can hammer in some nails or other small pointy objects into it in order to create a mace or spiked baseball bat. Most relatively smart attackers take one look at such an object and decide against trying to attack its wielder. While this type of item is more of a weapon than an overall tool, like a knife or a hammer, it is definitely effective.

If you are in your vehicle during a bug-out, you can also use your tire iron as a blunt weapon.

Tasers and Stun Guns

While knives and tools have multiple purposes, tasers or stun guns are generally used for the single purpose of defense. But they definitely increase your chance of survival if you are being attacked by a human or an animal.

However, it must be stated that this type of weapon can only help you so much. Bigger and more frenzied animals and humans tend to be much more resistant to the shock associated with tasers and stun guns than their smaller counterparts.

So, if you are being attacked by an animal, do not expect a weapon like this to save your life. They also probably will not win any long and drawn-out fights against humans, either.

If you do decide to use these as alternatives to guns, be sure to use them as a disabling measure rather than a fight-winning weapon. You should attempt to use the shocking power of the device to disable the animal or individual, so you can escape or grab a more serious weapon. Pepper sprays, mace, and wasp sprays also can provide similar types of defensive measures.

Note that tasers, stun guns, pepper sprays, or mace may be illegal in your area. Please check your local laws.

Air Guns

Unlike stun guns, tasers, and defensive sprays, air guns can actually have productive uses other than self-defense. If you decide to use something like a high-powered air rifle as your firearm alternative, there is a good chance that the air rifle will actually be able to kill small mammals and birds for food.

If you do choose to use an air rifle for this purpose, get a .177 or .22 caliber rifle. The .177 is easier to aim, but the .22 is better for hunting and stopping power. If you can get two rifles, consider adding a larger-caliber rifle, such as a .357.

Air rifles also have many other benefits. They are actually significantly less expensive than traditional firearms and also use less expensive ammunition. It is also certainly easier to obtain an air rifle than a traditional rifle. In most areas, an individual can purchase an air rifle without having to be the subject of a background check, and you usually do not have to fill out any annoying paperwork during the purchase process.

However, it is good to keep in mind that while the air rifle can be an incredibly useful firearm alternative, it is not easy to conceal, nor is it as silent as an edged weapon like a knife.

If you do want to conceal an air-based weapon, you can purchase a smaller weapon like an air pistol. However, you need to keep in mind that smaller-caliber air guns like air pistols will probably not kill any game mammals or birds. But air pistols can look remarkably similar to real handguns, so this type of weapon certainly has an intimidation factor when used

Air pistols usually aren't lethal, but their looks can be intimidating.

for defense. Last, despite the smaller caliber of air pistols, they can injure someone if fired at close range. This fact can make air pistols a good tool for slightly injuring attackers for disabling purposes or to encourage them to flee.

If you do choose to use an air gun, make sure you store plenty of ammunition with your prepping supplies. Also, your area may have legal restrictions against air guns. Please check your local laws.

Conclusion:
Keeping Your Family Safe

WE'VE COVERED A LOT OF INFORMATION IN THIS BEGINNING manual on survival prepping. But whether it's a natural disaster, a medical pandemic, a financial system collapse, a riot, or a societal breakdown, I have one final bit of advice for you.

When it comes to keeping your family safe, the most important concept to focus on is:

DON'T PANIC

Yes, natural disasters, pandemics, cyberattacks, riots, and even weather conditions are difficult situations to deal with. But widespread panic by those involved causes more harm than the original event does. If you can keep a cool head while everyone around you is panicking, you will have an advantage when it comes to survival.

I'm hoping by now that you look at, think about, and have a good feel for one simple fact . . .

You can survive and thrive in even the most difficult situations.

By taking the steps in this book, you'll not only be preparing yourself and your family physically. You'll be doing something even more important. You'll be preparing mentally and emotionally. You and your family will be developing the "survivalist" mind-set that will be far more valuable than any of your physical preparations.

This mind-set will not only serve all of you well during an emergency, but it will also contribute to your health and happiness in your regular, daily life.

That's one thing most new preppers are surprised to find once they get started. Rather than becoming scared and paranoid, you will feel the opposite way by prepping for survival. Survival prepping enhances and improves our lives physically and emotionally. It makes us appreciate all the things we do have and also gives us confidence as we go about our professional, domestic, and social lives.

And because of this confidence, it's not unusual to become more successful in life, to have higher self-esteem, and to be just a much happier person—all from getting involved in prepping.

I know that might sound weird to those outside the prepper movement, but to those of us on the inside, we know it's true. We've experienced it first-hand.

I hope I've inspired you to start taking those first steps toward survival preparation.

Thank you as always for taking the time to read my book. If you have any suggestions for improving this book, or for what you'd like to see in upcoming books, please feel free to email me at jason@adamsprep.com. You can also visit my website at AdamsPrep.com for more information.

I also need your help to spread the word about survival prepping in general and this book in particular. So if you liked this book, I'd appreciate it if you would tell your extended family and friends about it. Especially if it is someone you care about, you may want to purchase a copy of this book for them as a gift.

You can also help get the word out by telling others about this book on social media and by posting reviews about it on Amazon and other online book websites. Even if it's just a few words, your review helps bring survival prepping to those who might not have heard about it. Think of it this way—the more people you can help introduce prepping to, the better all of us will be able to survive and thrive in any difficult situations that come our way.

Thank you for all of your support. I wish you all the best for your new life as a prepper.

—Jason Ryder Adams
Forest Grove, Oregon

Appendix: Your Survival Plan Checklists

HERE ARE CHECKLISTS YOU CAN USE TO PUT TOGETHER YOUR BASIC emergency supplies for hunkering down, bugging out, and sealing in.

It might be easier to work with these lists if you have a printed copy, separate from this book. So to help you out, I can give you copies of these lists that you can print on your printer. Just go online and visit AdamsPrep.com.

Your Hunker-Down Supplies

Water
Store away from dangerous chemicals. Change out with fresh water every six to twelve months.

- ☐ Three gallons per person per day—store in containers and date each container
- ☐ Containers for water storage (55-gallon drums or other approved containers)
- ☐ Pans for boiling
- ☐ Camping water filter
- ☐ Distilling flask

☐ Chlorine bleach (unscented, 8.25 percent hypochlorite, label says suitable for disinfections and sanitation)

Food
Inspect every six to 12 months for expiration date.

☐ Enough food for three meals per day per person, plus snacks
☐ Canned meats, soups, chili, beans, and stews
☐ Canned fruits and vegetables
☐ Aseptic packaged soup, fruit juices, and drinks
☐ MRE packages, self-heating
☐ Dehydrated camping meals
☐ Peanut butter or other nut butters
☐ Snack bars made of granola, protein, or fruit
☐ Dry cereals or granola
☐ Dried fruit
☐ Shelled nuts
☐ Crackers that can substitute for bread
☐ Canned, pasteurized milk
☐ Vitamins and other dietary supplements
☐ Infant foods and formulas
☐ Comfort foods
☐ Charcoal stove (for outdoor use) or indoor propane stove
☐ Charcoal
☐ Lighter fluid
☐ Propane for indoor propane stove
☐ Spatulas for grill
☐ Grill cleaner

☐ Hot plate (if electricity is available)
☐ Paper towels
☐ Sharp knife
☐ Eating utensils—plastic knives, forks, spoons, plates, and cups
☐ Trash bags
☐ Can opener
☐ Dish soap

Hygiene

☐ Garbage bags for everyday waste
☐ Garbage bags for human waste (placed over toilet bowl)
☐ "Honey buckets" (special containers for storing waste)
☐ Quicklime to neutralize human waste
☐ Baking soda to neutralize human waste
☐ Specialized waste buckets
☐ Hand soap
☐ Alcohol-based sanitary wipes
☐ Toothbrushes and toothpaste
☐ Toilet paper
☐ Facial tissues

First Aid Kit

☐ First aid booklet
☐ Sterile gauze, both 2x2 and 4x4 sizes
☐ Medical tape—paper, silk, or plastic
☐ Adhesive bandages in multiple sizes
☐ Several rolls of three- or four-inch self-adherent elastic wrap
☐ Compression wraps—at least two four-inch wraps

- ☐ Several antiseptic wipes
- ☐ Antibacterial liquid soap
- ☐ Triple antibiotic ointment—preferably with lidocaine
- ☐ One bottle of hydrogen peroxide
- ☐ A tube of anti-itch cream
- ☐ One bottle of chewable aspirin tablets, commonly referred to as baby aspirin
- ☐ Tweezers
- ☐ Bandage scissors
- ☐ A few large safety pins
- ☐ Medical-grade cold compresses
- ☐ Calamine lotion
- ☐ Cotton balls
- ☐ One bottle of alcohol or a box of alcohol wipes
- ☐ Thermometer
- ☐ Latex gloves—use polyurethane or vinyl if you have a latex allergy
- ☐ Small flashlight with batteries
- ☐ Small box of diphenhydramine/antihistamine allergy tablets
- ☐ Tongue depressors
- ☐ Several bottles of water
- ☐ EpiPens for those with life-threatening allergies
- ☐ Over-the-counter NSAID medications (ibuprofen) and other pain relievers
- ☐ Up-to-date prescription medication for those with medical needs

Communications
- ☐ Corded, nonelectric phone attached to landline
- ☐ Cell phone and/or satellite phone

- ☐ External batteries or extra charged batteries for cell/ satellite phone (or solar cell phone charger)
- ☐ Battery-powered transistor radio or an NOAA Weather Alert Radio
- ☐ Extra batteries for radio (or solar-powered radio or hand-cranked radio)
- ☐ Ham radio, CB Radio, or walkie-talkies
- ☐ Backup batteries or backup generator for radios
- ☐ Printed or written list of all emergency contact phone numbers.

Children
- ☐ Diapers
- ☐ Toys, books, and entertaining diversions
- ☐ Favorite pillows, blankets, clothing

Pets
- ☐ Food and water
- ☐ Medicine
- ☐ Collar with ID
- ☐ Pet carrier
- ☐ First aid kit: cotton bandage rolls, tape, scissors, flea and tick prevention, gloves, a pet first aid book, antibiotic ointment and an isopropyl alcohol and saline solution
- ☐ Sanitation: litter, newspapers, trash bags, and bleach
- ☐ Toys
- ☐ Treats

General Equipment

- ☐ Flashlights—a battery-powered lantern is helpful for long power outages—extra batteries
- ☐ Whistle or personal siren—a loud noise can save lives in a debris field
- ☐ Infant supplies—diapers, baby wipes, fresh formula, medicine
- ☐ Air filtering materials—masks or cotton t-shirt to use as a breathing filter
- ☐ Shelter-in-place—plastic sheeting, scissors, and duct tape to cover doors and windows
- ☐ Tools to turn off utilities—wrench or pliers

Clothing and Bedding

Climate is a major consideration in the selection of clothing for the emergency kit. Power outages can remove the ability to heat and cool the interior of the home. Clothing and bedding must be replenished to adjust for growing children and new family members.

Clothes for EACH person must be included in the kit:

- ☐ A coat or jacket
- ☐ Long pants or jeans
- ☐ A long-sleeved shirt
- ☐ Sturdy walking shoes
- ☐ Hat and gloves
- ☐ Sleeping bag or warm blanket

Specialty Supplies

Certain situations will dictate the need for special equipment that will be helpful. As you build an emergency kit for your family, consider which of the items on this list would be helpful:

- ☐ Rain gear in wet climates
- ☐ Cash and change for immediate needs, including gasoline
- ☐ Paper towels
- ☐ Pencil and paper
- ☐ Tent
- ☐ Fire extinguisher
- ☐ Matches in a sealed container
- ☐ Compass
- ☐ Signal flare
- ☐ Feminine hygiene supplies
- ☐ Disinfectant
- ☐ Personal hygiene items
- ☐ Spare eyeglasses and/or contacts
- ☐ Medicine dropper
- ☐ Chlorine bleach—already mentioned under "Water" but a germ-killing cleaner for many uses.
- ☐ Books and other diversions for the adults
- ☐ Permanent marker (for labeling cans)

Home Equipment

- ☐ Generator (standby or portable)
- ☐ Gas for generators
- ☐ Extension cords for generators
- ☐ Heater—electric, kerosene, or propane
- ☐ Extra fuel for heaters
- ☐ Chainsaw
- ☐ Shovels and tools

☐ Work gloves

Your Bug-out Bag and Vehicle Kit Supplies Checklist

Bug-out Bag Checklist

☐ Water (as much as you can carry)
☐ Water bottle with built-in purifier/filter
☐ Water purifying tablets
☐ Ready-to-eat/self-heating camping meals
☐ Dehydrated food
☐ Food that bulks when cooked (rice, oatmeal)
☐ Energy bars and granola bars
☐ Nuts and dried fruit
☐ First aid kit
☐ First aid booklet
☐ Prescription medications
☐ Toothbrush and toothpaste
☐ Compact pop-up tent
☐ Sleeping bag
☐ Backpacking tent
☐ Sleeping bag
☐ Mess kit/cookware
☐ Utensil kit (knife, fork, spoon)
☐ Collapsible camping cup
☐ Flashlight or lantern and spare batteries
☐ Matches in sealed container
☐ Sharp hunting knife
☐ Backpacking saw
☐ Compass
☐ Sewing kit

- ☐ Work gloves
- ☐ Sunscreen
- ☐ Bug spray
- ☐ Rain gear (poncho and rain pants)
- ☐ Garbage bags
- ☐ Document case with legal and financial documents
- ☐ Cash (paper currency and coins)
- ☐ Keys (to home and bug-out location)
- ☐ Barter items (gold and silver bullion coins, numismatics, jewelry, additional supplies)
- ☐ Personal protection (pepper spray, gun, ammunition)
- ☐ Towel
- ☐ Washcloth
- ☐ Hand sanitizer
- ☐ Dry shampoo
- ☐ Biodegradable camping wipes (bathing substitute)
- ☐ Empty spray bottle (bathing substitute)
- ☐ Hiking toilet paper and biodegradable wipes
- ☐ Facial tissues (compact package)
- ☐ Hiking shoes or boots (not packed, but ready to put on and go)
- ☐ Foot cream and adhesive bandages

Vehicle Kit Checklist

- ☐ Additional water
- ☐ Additional food
- ☐ Canned meats, soups, chili, beans, and stews
- ☐ Canned fruits and vegetables
- ☐ Aseptic packaged soup, fruit juices, and drinks
- ☐ Can opener
- ☐ Small camping stove

- ☐ Lighter
- ☐ Matches in plastic, resealable bag
- ☐ Plastic utensils, bowls, cups
- ☐ Heavy-duty tent
- ☐ Heavier sleeping bags
- ☐ Tarp, rope, and stakes
- ☐ Vehicle fuel (store separately from kit, put in vehicle just before bugging out)

Additional Items for Children and Pets
- ☐ Children: Medication
- ☐ Children: Diapers
- ☐ Children: Wipes
- ☐ Children: Crackers
- ☐ Children: Change of clothes
- ☐ Children: A comfort blanket or toy
- ☐ Children: A pacifier
- ☐ Pet: Carrier or leash
- ☐ Pet: Backpack with harness
- ☐ Pet: Food
- ☐ Pet: Water
- ☐ Pet: Collapsible bowl
- ☐ Pet: Canned pet food
- ☐ Pet: Copy of pet's health records
- ☐ Pet: Photo of pet
- ☐ Pet: Flea and tick treatment
- ☐ Pet: Medications
- ☐ Pet: Favorite pet toy or blanket

Your Sealing In Checklist
- ☐ Duct tape

- ☐ Scissors
- ☐ Plastic sheeting (polyethylene sheeting; alternative: plastic garbage bags, plastic shower curtain liners, plastic drop cloths)
- ☐ Soap
- ☐ Alcohol-based hand sanitizer
- ☐ Toilet paper
- ☐ Facial tissues
- ☐ Deodorant
- ☐ Chlorine bleach and disinfectants
- ☐ Honey buckets or garbage bags for human waste
- ☐ Baking soda and/or quicklime
- ☐ HEPA filter (central or freestanding)
- ☐ Water—three gallons per day per person, 10-day supply minimum
- ☐ Food—10-day supply
- ☐ Can opener
- ☐ Eating utensils—plastic knives, forks, and spoons; plates; paper cups
- ☐ Dish soap
- ☐ First aid kit
- ☐ Bandages, cotton pads, elastic wraps, gauze, and medical tape
- ☐ Rubbing alcohol, peroxide, and witch hazel
- ☐ Aspirin
- ☐ Antidiarrhea medications
- ☐ Multivitamins
- ☐ Cough and cold medicines
- ☐ Prescription medications
- ☐ N95 masks

- ☐ Latex gloves—use polyurethane or vinyl if you have a latex allergy
- ☐ Toilet paper
- ☐ Deodorant
- ☐ Disinfectants
- ☐ Mobile/cell phone with external/spare charged batteries
- ☐ Transistor radio with batteries
- ☐ Flashlights or battery-powered lanterns, with extra batteries
- ☐ Baby wipes
- ☐ Toiletries (feminine products, shampoo, soap, shaving cream, and toothpaste)
- ☐ Diapers
- ☐ Infant formula
- ☐ Children's favorite pillows, blankets, clothing
- ☐ Tool Box
- ☐ Pet food and water
- ☐ Pet medicine, first aid kit, flea and tick treatment
- ☐ Pet litter, newspapers
- ☐ Pet toys and treats
- ☐ Board games and other entertainment
- ☐ Buckets, bottles, and containers

About the Author

JASON RYDER ADAMS IS THE LEADING EXPERT ON PRACTICAL survival prepping for "nonpreppers."

"Survival preppers are no longer weird nutcases living outside of society," says Jason. "We're normal people. We're your friends, your coworkers, and your neighbors. It's just that we're concerned for ourselves and for our families and want to make sure that we're prepared no matter what the world throws at us."

Jason emphasizes a down-to-earth approach to prepping.

"Let's face it, most people don't prep, and those that want to prep are overwhelmed by all the details involved. You start talking to someone new to prepping, and once you start in on the details, you see their eyes start to glaze over and their mouth drops and their face goes blank. It's just too overwhelming to the new prepper.

"I try to break down prepping into simple steps and make it as easy as possible for the new prepper to get started. After all, a little prepping is better than no prepping. And once people take those first few steps, they'll soon see that prepping isn't all that hard. And it will give them the confidence to go from being a little prepared to being fully prepared.

"If I had only one wish for you and for all of my readers, it's that you and they NEVER have to use what I write about.

"But these days, with everything going on in the world, I don't think that will happen. All of us are likely to face some sort of disaster at some point—whether it's natural or man-made. So I want you to be ready when it happens.

"Thank you as always for taking the time to read my books. I wish you and your family a healthy, happy, safe life."

You can contact Jason through his website at AdamsPrep .com.